BAPTISM IS
PRESENT TENSE

Foreword by: The Right Reverend Samuel Johnson Howard
Eighth Bishop to The Diocese of Florida

*An Episcopal
Guide To A
Sacrament That Is
Ever Before Us*

*For Baptismal
Candidates
and Small
Group Study*

PRESS

Baptism Is Present Tense:
An Episcopal Guide To A Sacrament That Is Ever Before Us
by The Reverend Ken Herzog

Printed in the United States of America

ISBN 9781498416177

Scripture quotations taken from the New Revised Standard Version (NRSV). Copyright © 1989 the Division of Christian Education of the National Council of the Churches of Christ in the United States of America.

Scripture quotations taken from the New American Standard Bible (NASB). Copyright © 1960, 1962, 1963, 1968, 1971, 1972, 1973, 1975, 1977, 1995 by The Lockman Foundation. Used by permission. All rights reserved.

www.xulonpress.com

FORWARD

When the Episcopal Church adopted a new Book of Common Prayer in 1979, it marked the conclusion of over two decades of serious theological and liturgical study. In many ways, the life of our church would never be the same again. As the words of our Book of Common Prayer changed, so too did the ways in which we worship. Indeed, our understanding of the rites of the Church was transformed. *Lex orandi, lex credendi:* An ancient principle of Christian life and worship that means, literally, "the law of prayer is the law of belief." It is a principle which those of us in the Episcopal Church have seen and experienced in our own lives over the past three and a half decades.

Our Prayer Book 1979 has changed the ways in which we look at our worship, how we address God, and how we relate to one another. In previous Books of Common Prayer, lay people had little or no role in worship. In our current prayer book, the role of lay people is greatly increased, lifting them to positions of real leadership in worship. Before the 1970s, the worship of most Episcopal churches followed an alternating pattern of Holy Eucharist and Morning Prayer at principal Sunday morning services. In many of our churches, therefore, Holy Eucharist was celebrated as the principal service only twice—and in some places, only once—a month. The 1979 Book of Common Prayer makes it clear that Holy Eucharist is to be the principal act of worship in each of our churches on every Sunday. Consequently, many of us today who previously considered communion once or twice a month to be adequate find ourselves feeling undernourished by Sunday worship which does not include the Eucharist.

Of all the changes in our life and worship engendered by the 1979 Book of Common Prayer, none is larger, more meaningful or more important than our understanding of Holy Baptism. When many of us were young, we referred to Holy Baptism as "Christening," and we understood it as a sweet— even nostalgic—family time in which parents, grandparents and godparents, together with a few close friends, gathered around the fount with the priest for brief and private prayers over a newborn. While the spiritual significance of Christening may have been great in the lives of those directly involved, its significance often did not resonate throughout the wider church.

All of that changed with our new Book of Common Prayer, which calls for the administration of Holy Baptism to be public, part of principal services of worship and participated in not only by the families and individuals involved, but also by all of the worshipping community gathered together. Our Church now views the sacrament of Baptism as it was always intended: a transformational moment of commitment and of blessing and a transformational event in the lives of all involved—the candidate for Baptism, friends, family, and the whole congregation.

It is this life-changing and transformational aspect of Baptism that my friend and colleague, Father Ken Herzog, has caught so well in his *Baptism Is Present Tense.* Working from Prayer Book and from Scripture, Father Herzog fills his study guide on Holy Baptism with engaging examples of how this sacrament is being lived out at its best in our Church today. He has written a book which is not only theologically instructive, but which can also assist clergy and laity alike in the preparation for and observance of the life-changing sacrament of Holy Baptism.

Ken Herzog has done a superb job of exploring and explaining Baptism in a highly readable and accessible manner. I commend *Baptism is Present Tense* to all who long for a deeper and more profound understanding of Baptism and of what it means to belong to the Church of Jesus Christ in which Baptism is the central act of initiation and acceptance.

The Rt. Reverend Samuel Johnson Howard
Bishop of the Episcopal Diocese of Florida
September 2012

I dedicate this work to the spirit of my wife, Elizabeth.

It is the Spirit of the Living God, the Holy Spirit
Who lives mightily within her.
It is what attracted me to her when we first met.
It is evidenced by her love of the Lord, her joy reflective in
her dynamic smile,
her unconditional love of our son and me,
her tenacity, resilience, and her deep compassion for those
who are hurting...
even little animals.
It is this spirit which will live forever which is
as long as I will love her.

Introduction

I have a good friend who is also an Episcopal priest. He preaches for 45 minutes every Sunday. This is an eternity in the Episcopal Church when you also take our liturgy into consideration. He jokes and tells his people to pack a lunch. I asked him about this one time and he told me that sermonettes make Christianettes. He was serious. He told me that if his people cannot be at Church long enough to hear a good sermon then they should question why they come at all. He was convincing and in the end I agreed with him, although I still preach for no more than the usual 12-14 minutes. I have always thought of the Mark Twain line that people's ability to listen to a sermon is directly proportionate to their ability to sit comfortably in a pew. When visiting a church, the first thing I look to see is whether or not the pews are padded.

However, my friend has a point and I am the first one to agree with him even though I practice the opposite. Do people go to Church out of obligation- just to put in their time? Does the IHS above the cross mean, "One Hour Service?" Do we seek to give the minimum to our Savior Who gave us everything? Sundays are not for us. Sundays are for God. Church is not something you do while you wait for your Sunday to unfold. Rather, you allow your Sunday to unfold after you have attended Church. I didn't understand this when I sat in the pew, but since being ordained, I understand it completely. Blessed are those parishioners who share this understanding. Parishes cannot exist without them. And doubly blessed are those parishioners who attend two services; those who sing in the choir at the 9:00 Service and then turn right around and sing again at the 11:15 Service, or the one who is a Lay Reader at one service and a Prayer Minister at the following one. These people get it. They understand.

It is in the same spirit that I undertake this writing about Baptism. Baptism is our first opportunity to be saved and Baptismal Preparation needs to be taken more seriously than it has in the past; at least in The Episcopal Church. It is not just a hoop through which to jump. Too often I have sat with people seeking Baptism who just want to go through the motions that will lead to the ceremony. As my friend explains about his sermons, perhaps they should question why they are there. If Candidates for Holy Baptism and their sponsors are not willing to make a commitment to proper Baptismal Preparation then are they ready to make the commitment to Baptism itself?

Baptism is the first step in the most important relationship in our life; our relationship with our Lord and Savior Jesus Christ. The Canons of the Episcopal Church state,

"It shall be the duty of Rectors or Priests-in-Charge to ensure that persons be prepared for Baptism. Before baptizing infants or children, Rectors or Priests-in-charge shall ensure that sponsors be prepared by instructing both the parents and Godparents for the Christian training of the

*baptized child, and how these obligations may
properly be discharged," (1).*

Is it too much to ask a Candidate for Holy Baptism and the sponsors to properly prepare for Baptism by reading a pamphlet of this length? I do not think so. Priests do not ask too much from our people. Most often we ask too little. There are many Episcopal Churches that demand much more and you must also consider that in the early Church, Baptismal Preparation lasted the entire Season of Lent (**Book of Common Prayer,** 265). If you are serious about Baptism, you will find these pages informative and foundational. There are various pamphlets written for Baptismal Preparation that are 5-10 pages in length that I have used on occasion. A quick read and away we go. Pamphlettes make Baptismettes. Jesus never took the easy way out simply because the stakes of salvation are too high.

I believe, *Baptism Is Present Tense* is a good preparation for this Holy Sacrament, but it is only a beginning and considering the true nature of Holy Baptism, there is nothing in a single volume that contains everything. That would be virtually impossible. Baptism is a lifelong journey and the journey is continually being written. The vows we make at Holy Baptism are something that must be practiced and worked out every day. As Paul writes, "See, now is the acceptable time; see, now is the day of salvation," (2 Corinth. 6:2b). And again, "...work out your own salvation with fear and trembling, (Phil. 2:12b). These verses are present tense because baptism is present tense..

This work is also intended to be a good resource for a small group study. A small group study was on the back burner as I was writing. I envision a group of Episcopalians using these writings as a tune up kit for their own spiritual walk; kind of like a "get back to basics" kit that will enliven their personal faith. If Baptism is present tense then we should presently be working on improving our spiritual lives.

Baptism is the Christian initiation into a relationship with the Lord. It is the reference point of the New Covenant. Too often people are baptized and then they leave their Baptism behind them, somewhere in the past never referring to it again. The opposite is true. Once you are baptized, your life alters its course and it takes a daily check to stay on course. Our Baptism is the reference point and measuring stick by which we judge the way we live.

I had an incredible experience regarding Baptism when I was 17 years old. I write about this in Section IX. From that point on I have put very small pieces of the puzzle together until I have reached the firm conclusions I have today. God's revelation has come to me slowly and my understanding about Baptism has been my own lifetime journey. I share it with you between the covers of this work.

It has taken two years for me to finish this work. Although I have always been inclined to write about this Holy Sacrament, I began after I had broken my collar bone in a motorcycle accident. Never one to sit around, I had to be doing something and so the Spirit helped me to piece together an outline and I began typing with one hand. It is fairly comprehensive in my understanding concerning this initial sacrament, and you will notice that the Holy Scriptures and The Book of Common Prayer are my two main sources. I have gone over and over each section making sure it correctly expresses my true beliefs and making sure that my beliefs are scripturally sound and in accordance with the Church's teachings. In that way it has been a case of ready...aim...aim...aim. There comes a time, however, when you just have to let the arrow fly...and this is it. Oddly enough, even though I insist that baptism is an action word, in this work, the word, "baptism" will be capitalized only when it is used as a noun in a direct reference to the Sacrament of Baptism; when you can commonly put the adjective, "Holy" in front of it. But it will not be capitalized for all other references.

I use storytelling to illustrate important points. I just told you one about a friend of mine. Stories make the faith personal. Stories help us find the sacred in the secular. It means that your spiritual antennas are up and that you are tuned in. This is very important. A daily prayer of mine is to ask God to help me find Him in the mundane world as I go about my day. I encourage you to join in that prayer if you are not already doing so. I am sure you have stories of your own and it is healthy to share them as a witness to the Risen Christ as you find Him in your life.

A good way to use this work as a preparation for Baptism is to read it in its entirety and then discuss the Overriding Questions in Section X with the one who will be performing the Baptism. A good way to use this work as a group study is to read each section individually and to use the 7 questions at the end of each section for discussion.

Finally, I want you to know how much I love the Episcopal Church. I found the Episcopal Church through my wife, Beth to whom I am truly grateful. I have found the living God through the Episcopal Church and no one person or group of people, and no one issue or groups of issues will ever chase me away from her. I'm all in. And in a very real way, this is my gift to her. It is with modest humility that I offer it.

Section I:

Baptism Is Present Tense

*B*aptism is present tense. I know that grammatically speaking, baptism is a noun and technically does not have a tense. My wife, Beth has been an upper school English teacher her entire professional life and she reminds me that baptism is a noun without a tense, but spiritually speaking baptism is an action word that carries the present tense.

When John the Baptist appeared in the desert and the people went out to him from Jerusalem and all the region of Judea, he said to them, *"I baptize you with water for repentance, but one who is more powerful than I is coming after me; I am not worthy to carry his sandals,"* (Matt. 3:11). In this case, I understand that grammatically speaking, *"baptize"* is the verb of this sentence. It is the action word. And this is a good start. But I am speaking more along the lines of what the Sacrament of Baptism implies in our everyday living. I am not speaking about the grammatical part of a sentence. I am speaking about the spiritual core of our relationship with the Lord. I am speaking of what Holy Baptism means for all Christians in the here and now, and what impact it has on every minute of every day. It is what keeps the Christian heart beating. Baptism is an action word which cannot be merely relegated as a subject or an object or the verb of a sentence.

We must say, "I am baptized." Using it in this way as my wife continues, "baptized" is an adverb which modifies the verb "am." But that's OK. Adverb is good. At least it is closer to the spiritual understanding that Baptism deserves. "I am baptized." It becomes a description of who I am. I am many things, and people use this phrase to describe many things; "I am very tired. I am very upset. I am in such a good mood. I am in love. I am the CEO of the company." But most importantly in the eyes of God, "I am baptized." Every time you look in the mirror you need to remind yourself of that. It's present tense. "I am tired. I am really happy. I am really upset" will all pass away and be replaced by other feelings and mood swings. Love may end. And you will not be the CEO of the company forever. But Baptism is forever. It is indelible. It is eternal.

We must be careful the way we say, "I was baptized," as in phrases such as, "I was baptized when I was ten years old" or, "I was baptized in the same church as my Dad." These are past tense; for to use it in this way refers only to a ceremony which took place at some point in your past as if to indicate that its significance was left there. But Baptism is more than just a ceremony. It is a present tense lifestyle.

Instead, we must say, "I am baptized," so that its relevance is constant and ever with us. We must use Baptism in this way because Baptism has a claim on every breath we take, every move we make, every thought we have, and everything we do; present tense. Just like some of us say, "I am male." And others say, "I am female." You would never say,

"I was male," as if you are no longer male. Or, "I was female," like you are no longer so. Males view the world as males and act accordingly. Females view the world as females and act accordingly. Baptized people view the world as being baptized and act accordingly. We encounter the world partially through our gender disposition and other genetic and environmental nuances, but even more so, Christians encounter the world through our Baptism, which supersedes everything else. This is part of what Paul means when he writes, *"As many of you as were baptized into Christ Jesus have clothed yourselves with Christ. There is no longer Jew or Greek, there is no longer slave or free, there is no longer male and female; for all of you are one in Christ Jesus,"* (Gal. 3: 27, 28).

Baptism becomes engrained in our personality; who we are, our perception of the world, and the way in which we encounter the world and its people. Through Baptism, our entire existence, our very core, and our reason for being are marked by the Anointed. It is the first step and reference point of our walk with Jesus Christ.

As you can see, Baptism has a much stronger, deeper, and more profound claim on our being then mere gender disposition, mood swings, or what position we hold in society. Unfortunately, many people judge their self-worth by the position they hold in society, by their title, wealth, or self-appointed importance. Baptism has a spiritual claim on our living that will be carried into eternity. We are not a body which has a spirit. We are a spirit wrapped in a body. Like a cannoli, the good stuff is in the middle. Gender is just part of the outer wrapping. Baptism is integral to our spiritual core. A cannoli without the filling would be tasteless.

The human body is 80% water (1). At Baptism, the water of our body is anointed by Holy Chrism and "...marked as

Christ own forever," (**Book of Common Prayer, 308**). As we go about day to day, we carry this anointed water with us. We are never without it. We become the anointed water and the anointed water becomes us. We are saturated in holy, anointed water. We become living fountains of holy water. Therefore, our Baptism is forever with us.

Baptism is not anything you can take off and set aside like a coat or a jacket. Once you are baptized, it is there to stay. It's not like you can see some intriguing temptation in which you want to participate and take off your Baptism for a period of time while you engage in the temptation expecting to find it when you return. You cannot do that. It is spiritually impossible. The truth is that you take your Baptism into that illicit activity and your Baptism becomes a duck out of water. As you sin, the holy, anointed water never leaves you.

As the water in the body is used throughout the day by sweating, exercising, evaporation, and general activities, we must constantly hydrate ourselves physically and spiritually. The medical profession tells us to drink plenty of liquids. In like manner, we must hydrate ourselves spiritually through prayer, reading the scriptures, bible study, and church worship. We must constantly gulp up our Baptism in our daily living.

Unfortunately, most of our time is spent satisfying the body and not enough time is spent satisfying the spirit. The spirit develops an incredible thirst for something meaningful. The body gets the entrée. The spirit gets the leftovers. We have things backwards. If we spent as much time in the spiritual world as we do in the physical one, we would all be walking saints and life would hold true meaning.

If there is a void in your life right now...and most assuredly there is; it's because you have been spending too much time in the physical world and not enough time in the spiritual one. Let me give you some spiritual advice here: attempting to find satisfaction in the physical world is futile because the physical world always wants more of the physical world. The physical realm is never satisfied. However, spending even the least bit of time in the spiritual world quenches a thirst deep inside. That is where our core resides. That is where Christ is found. In reality, every Christian should be experiencing a void in his/her life because Baptism does not reach its fulfillment until we reach the Kingdom. In the meantime, there is always a thirst for more of Jesus. There is always a desire to reach the next level.

Jesus tells the Samaritan woman at the well, *"Everyone who drinks this water will be thirsty again, but those who drink of the water that I will give them will never be thirsty. The water that I will give them will become in them a spring of water gushing up to eternal life," (*John 4: 13,14). This is the water of Baptism that we carry around with us. This is the difference between physical water and spiritual water. This is the thirst that Jesus can quench. Physical water will just lead us to being thirsty again. Tap into the life spring of your Baptism and satisfy the thirst forever.

Being baptized is to be tuned into the spiritual world. This is especially true in John's Gospel. One of the main distinctions between John's Gospel and the Synoptic Gospels is that in John, Jesus is constantly engaged in a conversation taking place on two levels; one physical and one spiritual. The conversation He has with the Woman at the Well (John 4:4-42) is a classic example. The woman is talking about physical water and Jesus is talking about spiritual water; the water of Baptism. In John's Gospel, Jesus has similar conversations with Nicodemus about Baptism (John 3), with His disciples about the Bread of Life (John 6: 25-59), and again with His disciples about Lazarus sleeping (John 11). In each example, Jesus is teaching on a much deeper level than the one to whom He was speaking. He was calling them to something more profound, but each person was blind and deaf to the deeper meaning.

Being baptized is to come to understand that there is always, and I mean ALWAYS something going on in the spiritual realm. God is always, eternally at work with us. We just don't see Him. People speak of having a "God Moment," those times when they actually recognize His presence in a particular time. They say, "God really revealed Himself to me there." We often think that God opens Himself up to us during those times when the truth is that God is always present, it's just during those times we open ourselves up to Him. He is always there. Unfortunately, we are not. We are the yo-yos in this relationship. We are the ones who come and go. God is like a radio wave; always broadcasting...WGOD...100,000 watts of almighty power. But we control the on/off switch, the station selector, and the volume control.

I was once at the check- out- line of a grocery store. The check-out-girl asked me if I had a store discount card for the groceries I had purchased. Of course, I did not. There was an elderly lady right behind me who said to the girl, "Here, let him use mine." She had a warm smile on her face and I politely thanked her. The total then left me nine cents short of having to break another dollar. I pulled out my wallet to retrieve another dollar when the same lady handed over a dime. She had the same warm smile. I said, "Well, God has put me right in front of an angel today!" The lady responded, "As long as you recognize us when you see one!"

Instances like this one can happen all of the time if we are just tuned in. Not that people will go around doing us favors and giving us money, but that we can find the sacred in the secular. The truth is that God was with me every step I took in that grocery store and there could have been other opportunities in the store to encounter Him if I were not so blind. Like a tennis match, sometimes God aces us and passes by without our recognition because we are paying more attention to the groceries than to Him. These "holy moments" are the result of opening yourself up to God, giving Him permission to surface, and finding Him in the mundane routine of life, like picking up a few items at the grocery store. God is there anyway. You may as well invite Him in. It all starts with your Baptism and recognizing that Baptism is present tense.

Baptism is present tense because it is a constant call on our hearts for something deeper. It is not satisfied in the surfaced, material world perceived by the senses where empty dreams lay waste in the void of not being fulfilled. Baptism is not at home in the material world. Rather, Baptism is a dynamic call to living waters which can only be quenched through the desire of eternity. Eternity is where Baptism points and its goal is unity with the Father through the Son in the Kingdom.

Baptism is present tense because it is a constant call to imitate Christ.

"Let the same mind be in you that was in Christ Jesus, who, though he was in the form of God did not regard equality with God as something to be exploited, but emptied himself, taking the form of a slave, being born in human likeness. And being found in human form, he humbled himself and became obedient to the point of death – even death on a cross. Therefore God also highly exalted him and gave him the name that is above every name, so that at the name of Jesus every knee should bend, in heaven and on earth and under the earth, and every tongue should confess that Jesus

Christ is Lord to the glory of God the Father,"
(Philippians 2: 5-11).

Servanthood...humility...obedient unto death. Paul opens this passage by instructing us that our attitude should be the same as Jesus...a humble servant who remained obedient unto death. Now, talk about a job description of a Christian. Baptism is present tense because this is a full time job. More than anyone, Jesus understood that He was a spirit wrapped in a body. We must not only think this way at the Baptismal Ceremony, but everyday thereafter. This is why Baptism is present tense. This must be our attitude. And it is not easy.

When I was single and living alone, I was a neat and tidy young man. I did the dishes everyday after dinner, vacuumed my small apartment, washed the kitchen floor on a regular basis, and kept up with the laundry. I thought I was doing OK. But when I met Beth...she introduced a whole new level of cleanliness. Everything was cleaner, brighter and shinier.

One day she brought over her high powered vacuum cleaner and started vacuuming my carpets. I couldn't believe it. With every stroke there was this gurgling noise as her machine was sucking up stuff in my carpet undetected by the naked eye. I watched in amazement. My eyes could not believe my ears. Then she licked her index finger and walked around the tile nabbing little paper scraps that even the high powered vacuum cleaner couldn't pick up. Give me a break! The future of our relationship was in jeopardy as I knew I could never live up to her standard of cleanliness. My facial expression must have been reflecting this incredulous disbelief I was experiencing when she looked me in the eye and said, "Don't worry. I'll teach you." I thought, "O boy! She is going to teach me! What a comfort. What peace!" The weight of the world was just lifted off of my shoulders. Beth is going to show me how to become a neat geek. There must be a God! When is the first lesson?

So here we are after 28 years of marriage. Our new, super high powered vacuum cleaner is less than a year old and it is going in for its 25,000 mile servicing. Our dog has learned to stay clear of it. I have learned that the cleaner things are, the stronger our marriage becomes. When our son was an infant he never sucked his thumb, but he developed this disgusting habit of licking his index finger. I am still far from where she is but further along from where I use to be.

All Christians undergo a similar spiritual experience. We think that we are doing a good job. We pray, read the bible, go to church, lend a hand when asked, and smile at people we don't even know. We feel good about ourselves. But then we look at Jesus and He introduces a whole new level of holiness. When you read the Gospels in light of the high powered vacuum cleaner, you get swept away by the way He led His life. How could He not worry about material things? (Matthew 6: 25-34). How did He love everyone, hate no one and not judge others? (Luke 8: 27-38). How could He be so understanding when one of His closest friends betrayed Him? (Mark 14: 27-31). How could He keep His cool when Pilate was in His face? (John 18: 28-40). And most of all, how could He pray for those driving in the nails? (Luke 23:34).

Think of these events. Think of these events and go back to Paul's words, "Your attitude must be the same as Christ Jesus..." All of a sudden, smiling at people I don't even know isn't such a big deal. Being a Christian is quite a challenge. It is a full time 24/7 job. It's downright difficult. Like I said, Baptism is present tense.

But who can measure up? No one can. I can't measure up to my wife's cleanliness or Jesus' holiness. But we must not get discouraged from trying. Not to try is to settle for mediocrity. If you aim at nothing you are bound to hit it (2). And comparing yourself to others only leads to resentment and a grudge (3). We must always strive for perfection, for by doing so we will always improve. Jesus is perfect and His attitude is perfect. As long as your attitude is that of a humble, obedient servant then your actions should follow, or at least more of them then if your attitude was something different.

Baptism is present tense because we need to constantly remind ourselves that Jesus is our model:

- He understood that He was a spirit wrapped in a body
- He did not worry about material possessions
- He loved everyone, hated no one, and did not judge anyone
- He was merciful and understanding when He was slighted
- He prayed for His enemies.

We can start there. That is certainly enough to keep us busy. We must strive to view the world as Jesus viewed the world. Probably by now you are beginning to realize that Baptism is more than you imagined. Do not be discouraged. You are on the path that will lead to the Kingdom and it greatly pleases God that you have begun this journey. It will add richness to your everyday life. It is not always easy because we attempt to fit the spiritual world into the temporal world. It takes time to learn how to view things from a different perspective, but you can do it, with God's help. By the way, the dust particles on the floor remind me that it's time to vacuum again. Baptism is present tense.

Questions

1. Assuming that you agree with the premise that "Baptism is Present Tense," how can this enrich your daily walk with the Lord?
2. For a person who does not agree with this premise, what other premise or premises about Baptism would be appropriate?
3. If the body is just the outer wrapping and the spirit lies at the core of who we are as a child of God then what percentage of your day is consumed with the outer wrapping and what percentage is consumed with the inner core?
4. Are you experiencing a void in your life right now? If so, what do you think contributes to this void and how can this void be overcome?
5. If our bodies are 80% water, how do you quench your spiritual thirst?
6. How often do you find the sacred in the secular?
7. How can you better have the mind of Christ?

Section II

Baptism is the
Sign of a New Covenant

*"Do not think I have come to abolish
the law and the prophets.*

*I have come, not to abolish them, but to fulfill them,"
(Matt. 5: 17).*

Everything in the Old Testament is fulfilled in the New Testament. This theme of fulfillment dominates the scriptures. There is always a foreshadowing. Like one of those pointer dogs, everything in the Old Testament points to something in the New.

Let me give you some examples:

The creation of the world in the Book of Genesis is fulfilled
    by the new heavens
and the new earth in the Book of Revelation.

The first man, Adam…sinned. So God recreates the world
spiritually through the Second Adam, Jesus, Who saves
us from our sins.

The Old Testament story of Noah and the Ark "points to"
Jesus and the Church.

The Ten Commandments of the Old Testament are fulfilled by
The Eight Beatitudes in the New Testament.

The Promised Land of the Old Testament is the physical land
of Canaan.

The Promised Land of the New Testament is the Kingdom.

The Sabbath becomes Sunday.

The altar of sacrifice becomes the altar of celebration.

The Passover Meal becomes the Last Supper which was the
First Eucharist.

Shepherds become bishops.

Rabbis become priests.

And faithful followers become disciples.

Everything in the Old Testament is fulfilled in the New
Testament.

In this light, circumcision in the Old Testament is fulfilled
by Baptism in the New Testament. All of scripture is centered
around two covenants: The Old Testament Covenant was
made between God and Abraham while The New Testament
Covenant is made between Jesus and us. One is built upon the
other. First, the Covenant with Abraham:

*"The Lord said to Abram, 'Go forth from the land of your
kinsfolk and from your father's house to a land that I will
show you. I will make of you a great nation, and I will bless
you. I will make your name great, so that you will be a
blessing. I will bless those who bless you and curse those*

> *who curse you. All the communities of the earth shall*
> *find a blessing in you" (Genesis 12: 1-3).*

"God also said to Abraham, 'On your part, you and your
descendants after you must keep my covenant throughout
the ages. This is my covenant with you and your descen-
dants after you that you must keep: every male among you
shall be circumcised. Circumcise the flesh of your foreskin,
and that shall be the mark of the covenant between you and
me. Throughout the ages, every male among you, when he is
eight days old, shall be circumcised, including house born
slaves and those acquired with money from any foreigner
who is not of your blood. Yes, both the house born slaves and
those purchased with money must be circumcised. Thus my
covenant shall be in your flesh as an everlasting pact.
If a male is uncircumcised, that is, if the flesh of his foreskin
has not been cut away, such a one shall be cut off from his
people; he has broken my covenant'" (Genesis 17: 9-14).

Abraham is the first real historical person in the bible and
he appears approximately 1800 B.C. (1). The promises God
made to him were important for a man in his culture. A long
life, many children, leaving an inheritance, and a well-known
name were considered to be signs of God's blessings; that
you were walking righteously and that you had earned God's
favor. Anyone lacking in these areas was looked down upon
and considered to be less favorable in God's eyes. You would
not want your child playing with the children of such parents.

Abraham's part of the covenant was obedience and trust.
God told Abraham to leave his home, his extended family, his
fortunes, and his livelihood, and to travel to a land God would
show him. Obedience and trust were essential in Abraham's

relationship with God. To mark his intention to enter into this covenant and as the first sign of obedience, Abraham was circumcised. Circumcision was a sign that Abraham desired to enter into this relationship with God. As God would remain faithful to Abraham, circumcision was a mark that Abraham planned to remain faithful to God. It was something Abraham had to do in order to establish his end of the covenant with God. While circumcision was already present in some tribal communities prior to the time of Abraham (2), God uses this procedure to mark the covenant with the Father of the Faith.

It is interesting that there are modern day medical pros and cons to circumcision. Religiously speaking, only Jews and Muslins require it by faith and while Abraham was told to circumcise on the eighth day, most infant males are circumcised earlier (3). The number of circumcisions worldwide is diminishing. The United States leads the world in the percentage of infant males who are circumcised and the vast majority of those are done for non-religious reasons. Most of these parents do not want their son to look differently in the shower when they take gym and play sports (4).

So are we losing the importance of the covenant that God made with Abraham? Apparently so. It does not seem necessary in a world becoming increasingly secular and less sacred; at least in the ancient traditions of the faith. The discussion of circumcision has turned into a discussion of body mutilation and disfiguring the gentiles to no significant advantage. Besides, our theology has changed as well. As God rewarded Abraham with material gifts, we have come to see that people who are faithful to God do not always prosper in the material world and unfaithful people do not always incur disaster. The Book of Job was partially written to dispel this myth (5). Do not bad things happen to good people? Four thousand years after Abraham, how God works in the world is just as much of a mystery as it was back then; if not more so. Mystery begins where knowledge leaves off and there are many aspects of God which remain a mystery. The mind of God is so far above us that we can never understand. Our job is to trust and remain faithful. God's job is just to be God.

***

Baptism is the New Testament fulfillment of circumcision and it is the mark of the New Covenant with Jesus. The New Covenant with Jesus leads to salvation. *"The one who believes and is baptized will be saved; but the one who does not believe will be condemned," (Mk. 16:16).* To mark his/her intention to enter into this covenant with Jesus and as the first sign of obedience, a person must be baptized. As Jesus will remain faithful to the one who is baptized, Baptism is a mark that the person will remain faithful to Jesus. It is something that a person must do in order to establish his/her end of the New Covenant.

Like the covenant made with Abraham, God still demands a life of obedience and trust, but with Jesus, the rewards are not material, but spiritual. Jesus promises life in the Spirit, a life in the deeper realm of the spiritual world and eventually, the Kingdom. And as God made it clear with Abraham that an uncircumcised male will be cut off from God's people, Jesus makes it clear that unless you are baptized you cannot reap the benefits of God's faithfulness. *"Very truly, I tell you, no one can enter the Kingdom of God without being born of water and the Spirit," (Jn. 3:5).* There is no wiggle room here. So what happens when a baby is still born, or when an infant dies prior to being baptized, or someone living in a remote part of the world has never heard the Good News? Fortunately that is not our call. Our job is to trust and remain faithful. God's job is just to be God.

***

It is important to understand that circumcision for Abraham and Baptism for a Christian are signs which point to a deeper reality. Neither are ends in themselves. They do not stand alone. For Abraham, circumcision meant that he would vow his life to obedience and to trust God's will. For a Christian, Baptism is a sign of a lifetime of the same obedience and to trust God's Will. That is why Baptism is present tense; because we are constantly living into it. Obedience and trust in God's will is something which claims every waking moment of our lives.

As Abraham could not follow his own will and expect God to remain faithful simply because he was circumcised, neither can a Christian follow his/her own will and expect Jesus to remain faithful just because he/she is baptized. Of this reality, John the Baptist warned the Pharisees and Sadducees when they came to him to be baptized.

> *"You brood of vipers! Who told you to flee from the wrath to come? Give some evidence that you need to reform. Do not presume to say to yourselves, 'We have Abraham as our ancestor;' for I tell you, God is able from these stones to raise up children to Abraham," (Matt. 3:7-9).*

If you read between the lines, I believe you will find that John explains that circumcision is also present tense; that

Jewish authorities could not hang their hats on the simple fact that they were circumcised. Circumcision was a starting point but a necessary step for Abraham. Baptism is a starting point but a necessary step for a Christian.

So if circumcision is necessary to be included in the Covenant with Abraham and Baptism is necessary to be included in the Covenant with Jesus, and Baptism is the fulfillment of circumcision, then is it necessary for a new male convert to Christianity seeking Baptism to first be circumcised? In other words, is it necessary to be connected to Abraham's Covenant in order to be connected to Jesus' Covenant? This is an interesting question and one which spurred a heated debate in the early Church.

One could argue, "Yes" and not be totally wrong. The New Testament draws its roots from the Old Testament. Christianity evolved out of Old Testament Israel. Many people mistakenly believe that the opposite of Christianity is Judaism; far from it. Old Testament Jews are our relatives. If you read the New Testament without understanding the Old Testament, then that would be like arriving to a movie half way through. The plot and the characters lack real depth and meaning. The story line would be difficult to figure out. If you read the Old Testament without the New, it would be like arriving at the movie on time but having to leave half way through. You would wonder how it ends. Of course, you want to arrive on time and stay until the end.

Jews and Christians are relatives.

The New Testament draws its roots from the Old Testament.

Everything in the Old Testament is fulfilled in the
New Testament.

The other side of this discussion regarding circumcision and Baptism is to argue, "No, circumcision is not necessary in order to be baptized." In Biblical times, most converts to Christianity were formerly Jewish so it seemed natural to some of the early disciples that first becoming Jewish would be a proper progression. But the Gentiles, who were neither Jewish nor Christian, had never lived in the Jewish faith, so it seemed burdensome for them to first be circumcised in order to be baptized. Granted they should be instructed in the faith, but not enter into the Old Covenant that had already been renewed and fulfilled by Jesus Christ. Why go backwards? It is a New Covenant based on the Son of God Who was yet to be revealed in the Old Testament. Some of the early disciples viewed circumcision as an unnecessary step.

This was the heated argument among our early leaders and it included Peter, Paul, James, Barnabas, Simeon and others. It is laid out in Acts 15.

"Then certain individuals came down from Judea and were teaching the brothers, 'Unless you are circumcised according to the custom of Moses, you cannot be saved.' And after Paul and Barnabas had no small dissention and debate with them, Paul and Barnabas and some of the others were appointed to go up to

Jerusalem to discuss this question with the apostles and the elders" (Acts 15: 1,2) (6).

This resulted in the first Church Council called, "The Council of Jerusalem" which met in 50 A.D. in the City of Jerusalem. The Council decided upon the latter as Peter cites that we are saved only by the grace of Jesus Christ (Acts 15:4), and James decided that circumcision was not necessary for the Gentiles, but they should respect The Law of Moses by observing some of its core principles (Acts 15: 20). This was the beginning of proper Baptismal Instruction.

The transition from Judaism to Christianity is tighter than most people think. I have known families that have one parent who is Christian and the other who is Jewish. What a great opportunity for the children! They get the best of both worlds. Through each parent, the children can learn how the History of Salvation has unfolded. By attending the synagogue and the church, they are given a unique vantage point of scriptural fulfillment. By celebrating the Holy Days of both faiths, they participate in 4000 years of God's dwelling among His people.

Baptism is a sign that God is ready to take His relationship with His people to the next level by the promise of the Kingdom. The Baptism of an individual is a sign that he/she is also ready to take his/her relationship to the next level through a life of trust and obedience. Baptism is a sign of the New Covenant, not the end of the old one. Through Baptism, the individual becomes spiritually connected to the Covenant of Abraham whether a male has been circumcised or not. Baptism is not the end of the parents' responsibility toward their child. It is only the beginning. For an adult, Baptism is the alignment of your life to God's life through His Son, Jesus Christ. Baptism is present tense because this doesn't happen in a single ceremony, but a life long journey learning how to obey and to trust the Lord God. Baptism is a sacrament that we live into on a daily basis. We are never quite there and we will never be there until we reach the Kingdom where all of this is headed.

Your Baptism connects you to all of Salvation History. Your Baptism connects you to Jesus' Baptism. It connects you to the ministry of John the Baptist. It connects you to Abraham who lived 4,000 years ago. It's amazing to think that you are so connected to all of God's holy work in the world. And now you are part of it. It is as though Abraham, John, and Jesus will be in attendance. At your Baptism, they will be the honored guests.

Questions

1. The question is not, "Are you connected to the History of Salvation?" Because you are. The question is rather, "How aware are you that you are connected?"
2. Abraham was obedient to God and trusted in Him even though he had very little knowledge of God with which to direct his life. Knowing what you know about God, how obedient and trusting are you in your relationship with Him?
3. While striving to live a life of obedience and trust, do you still expect God to reward you materially? Are you disappointed that Jesus promises spiritual rewards and not material ones?
4. Would you rather live in the time of the apostles and see Jesus face to face but not have such revelation available to you, or would you rather live in the present day, not see Jesus but have the revelation available to you?

5. What does it mean that we are constantly living into our Baptism?
6. If you attended The Council of Jerusalem, would you have voted that Gentiles must first be circumcised before being baptized, or would you have thought that it was an unnecessary step? Support your answer.
7. Christianity evolved out of Old Testament Judaism. When you read the bible, do you consciously strive to understand the biblical fulfillments?

Section III:

The Baptismal Vows

*I*t is important to distinguish what Baptism is and what it is not. The Church is working very hard to dispel any myths associated with the Sacrament of Baptism. It is the main purpose of this writing. This initial sacramental step in the life of a new Christian needs to be better understood so that it can be assured that all baptized Christians have the proper mindset. I will begin with a few false assumptions which can alter the true meaning of the covenant.

Baptism is **NOT** just a nice ceremony to be followed by a nice reception. With some people the reception can overshadow the Baptism itself. In cases of infant Baptism, the baby is normally tired after the ceremony and after returning to the house, the baby is put down for a nap while the family celebrates, but sometimes the cause of the celebration is lost while catching up on each other's lives. This is not all bad for new life in Christ is a source of unity and celebration, however, families must be careful to keep the main thing the main thing.

The Sacrament of Holy Matrimony often suffers the same corollary. The engaged couple and their families become more concerned about the wedding than the marriage. A wedding and reception are for a day; a marriage is for a lifetime, and as long as the two are put into perspective then everything is fine.

In like manner, the Baptismal Ceremony and reception are for a day, but the covenant entered into at Baptism will remain for a lifetime. Notice that the scriptures surrounding the circumcision of Abraham and his household make no mention of a reception. While the need to celebrate is perfectly human, the secular should not outshine the spiritual. While planning the reception, efforts should be made to keep the spiritual in the center of everything.

Baptism is **NOT** an enrollment into some eternal insurance policy in the sky so that when the baptized person dies and reaches the Pearly Gates, his/her name is pulled up on the Almighty Computer Screen to see if there is a check mark out in the left hand column. While running the risk of sounding too blunt while making this point, I know from experience how easily this attitude can dominate the good intentions of the parents. The Church is working very hard to dismiss this attitude and rework our approach to this Holy Sacrament and this would be a good starting point.

Coupled with the above mentioned myth is the idea that Baptism fulfills the parents' spiritual responsibilities toward their child. This is not true. Sometimes there is a parental sigh of relief now that Junior is baptized. "We've done our job. People will now recognize us as good parents." There can even be undue pressure by grandparents to have Junior baptized. On the contrary, Baptism is one of the initial steps the parents take. It becomes part of the lifelong commitment parents make to their child along with love, food, water, and shelter; and not only part, but Baptism is the central part. Baptism brings with it a further determination on the part of the parents and god-parents to raise their child in the faith to know and love their Savior, Jesus Christ. Too often we will baptize Junior and never see him or his family again.

Baptism is **NOT** a spiritual bubble which will prevent the baptized from facing the difficult side of life. We are not promised a bed of roses. We only have to look at the life of Christ as an example. *"If anyone would come after me, he must deny himself and take up his cross and follow me,"* (Mark 8:34). The cross to which Jesus refers partially consists of the trials and tribulations of life. During very trying times, people sometimes become angry with God as though they are receiving unjust treatment. They feel as though their spiritual life, beginning with their Baptism, should somehow protect them from tragedy. This just isn't so. Abraham was not prom-ised a troubled free life and neither are we. Through Baptism, the disappointments and heartaches in our lives can be linked to the disappointments and heartaches in the life of Jesus and laid at the foot of the cross for final victory.

Baptism is not just a ceremony and reception. It is not an enrollment into an eternal insurance policy. It does not ful-fill the parents' spiritual responsibility to their child. And it is not a spiritual bubble of protection. Baptism **IS** a commit-ment, a covenant with the Almighty to be taken as seriously as Abraham viewed his covenant. It begins a life of trust and obe-dience. It would be wonderful if every Candidate for Baptism and/or the parents would first read Dietrich Bonheoffer's **The Cost of Discipleship** (1), especially the chapter on Cheap and Costly Grace. In part it reads:

"Cheap grace is the preaching of forgiveness without repentance, Baptism without church discipline, absolution without confession. Cheap grace is grace without discipleship, grace without the cross, grace without Jesus Christ. Costly grace calls us to follow, and it is grace because it calls us to follow Jesus Christ. It is costly because it costs a man his life, and it is grace because it gives a man the only true life. It is costly because it condemns sin, and it is grace because it justifies the sinner. What has costs God much cannot be cheap for us" (pgs. 44, 45).

Reading this book in its entirety would dispel any baptismal myth and set a proper course of understanding. However, seeing that this is not practical, a review of the Baptismal Vows is in order.

Godparents/Sponsors

Although the norm is two, each candidate for Holy Baptism must have at least one godparent or sponsor who is baptized. Even three is acceptable. When Jesus sent out His disciples into the world, He sent them out in pairs (Luke 10: 1). Two is the customary number in scripture for a witness. You always see two Jehovah's Witnesses at your door, never one and never three.

The number is not as important as the quality. The godparent or sponsor should be one who will take an interest in the life of one being baptized. Remembering a birthday and other significant life events, offering encouragement, being there during difficult times, and watching over one's spiritual life are all important roles. Godparents should buy a bible or some other spiritual gift to commemorate such events. Too often parents pick family members to fulfill these roles without seriously considering the responsibility involved. Godparents and sponsors should be able to properly answer and agree with the questions in The Baptismal Covenant.

The Questions of the Covenant

In the Episcopal Church, the Baptismal Covenant centers around six important questions located in **The Book of Common Prayer** on page 302. The questions are addressed to both the parents and the godparents.

Q 1. *Do you renounce Satan and all the spiritual forces of wickedness that rebel against God?*

A. *I renounce them.*

This first question takes for granted that the baptized, the parents, and godparents all believe that Satan exists and thus, hell exists as well. Too often these questions are answered with a polite, "I do" without the candidate and sponsors seriously considering the question. To answer this question correctly, the parties involved must recognize that there is a force of evil at work in the world. Not to do so plays right into Satan's hand. He knows that deep inside people do not want to deal with the dark side of life and so Satan is able to go to work without being noticed. He is the master of disguise and deceit. He would much rather that we blame God for the evil things we do and have happen to us, and many times we fall right into his trap.

To renounce Satan is not to deny his existence. Rather, it is to first recognize that he exists and that he is the source of evil in the world. He must not go unchecked. The candidate must get this part of his/her spirituality out in the open. He/she must confront the evil one so to put him in his place. Jesus makes references to Satan throughout the Gospels, but one of the best examples of Satan's work is explained by Jesus in The Parable of the Sower, *"Some people are like seed along the path where the word is sown. As soon as they hear it, Satan comes and takes away the word that was sown in them,"* (MK. 4:15). Satan is the master of nipping good things in the bud. Recognizing the presence of Satan is to understand that there is a battle being fought for your heart between Jesus and Satan, and both think that you are worth it. Jesus wants to save you and Satan wants to destroy you. This is the essence of spiritual warfare.

The question often surfaces, "So why does God allow Satan to exist?" The answer quite simply is free will. The basic choices in life are good and evil. God is the Source of goodness and Satan in the source of evil. The word "god" is a Greek word which means, "good." But God as we know Him, is the Source of everything that is good. The word, "Satan" on the other hand has Greek and Hebrew roots and simply means, "adversary." Satan opposes everything for which God stands. There has to be a source of evil in the world for us to be free. God could have created the world without evil and then we would be all good, but not free. God would rather allow evil to exist and have us be free than for us to be all good and not free. God makes Himself vulnerable for our freedom.

It is like someone you love. Would you rather have that person with you because he/she chooses to be with you, or because he/she is forced to be with you? I think you would prefer the former; and so does God. Instead of eliminating evil altogether and forcing us into a relationship with Him because there is no other option, God prefers to give us a choice and have us in a relationship with Him because we choose to be there. Have you freely chosen to have a relationship with the One Who created you? If you have not made this decision as of yet, now is a great time to do so.

In the end, however, God will conquer Satan and put an end to his power. Satan may win some battles but God will win the war. Satan knows that his time is limited and thus, he works furiously with the time he has. *"Be sober, be watchful. Your adversary the devil prowls around like a roaring lion, seeking someone to devour. Resist him, firm in your faith,"* (1 Peter 5: 8,9).

Did God create Satan evil? No! God creates only good things. *"God looked at everything He made and saw that it was very good,"* (GN. 1:31). God created Satan good, but Satan rebelled. Satan wanted to be like God so he fashioned his own domain; the domain which stands against everything good. Satan is the god of evil; the prince of darkness. Do you renounce him? If so, you have answered the first question correctly.

Q 2. *Do you renounce the evil powers of this world which corrupt and destroy the creatures of God?*

A. *I renounce them.*

This second question is more earthly than the first and easier to answer. Once the power of Satan is recognized then we can begin to understand how he works in the world in which we live. In short, anything which opposes goodness is Satan's work. Perhaps Satanic Cults would come to mind when considering this question. But Satan's attack comes on many fronts. The evil powers which destroy humans take center stage since humans are created in God's image. Physical destruction such as fighting, bodily harm, child abuse, murder, and war are all fall under this umbrella. Political regimes which rule by domination, control, fear and oppression, and dictators who care little about human dignity and equality must be stopped. But also, emotional and sexual abuse are part of this as well. Degradation, deceit, division, anger and hatred, prejudice, undermining, manipulation, revenge, neglect, selfishness and apathy toward the needs of others are also destructive powers toward humans. Anything which inflicts pain on the lives of others is the work of the evil one and must be renounced.

Satan does not stop with humans, however. Animal cruelty, destruction and pollution of our environment, arsonists, insensitivity toward wildlife, littering, not protecting animals on the verge of extinction, abuse of natural resources, and wasting food all serve no other purpose than to feed into Satan's plan of destruction. He is not picky as to who, what, and where to attack. It becomes easy to understand the magnitude of Satan's destructive powers and the wide range of battlefronts on which he engages. He is one busy dude. These are all destructive powers which must be renounced. Through Baptism, Christians have our hands full. Baptism is present tense.

Q 3. *Do you renounce all sinful desires that draw you from the love of God?*

A. *I renounce them.*

While the first question dwells on the existence of Satan and the second one paints in broad strokes his destructive powers in the world, this third question becomes very personal. This question probes your very heart to examine how Satan might be working in you as an individual.

The word, "sin" is a Greek word and has its roots in archery. When an archer shot his arrow and missed the target entirely, it was scored a "sine'." The word literally means, "to miss the mark" (2). To sin is to miss the mark of the vision God had for you when He created you. Anything which opposes God's vision for your life is the work of the evil one. Sin is a rebellion against God and sin in any form is unacceptable. Sin is self-destructive because it severs the bond between you and God.

The most serious offenses are called The Seven Deadly Sins. They are: false pride, anger, lust, greed, laziness, gluttony and jealousy. These are motives of actions which are very destructive and carry serious moral weight.

> *False pride* is arrogance and boastfulness and is the antithesis of humility. False pride takes personal credit for the gifts and blessings given by God.
>
> *Anger* is an emotion which opposes the love of God and often leads to violence. While Jesus often gets angry in the Gospels, He does not allow it to become destructive. Anger is a cycle which can easily become a generational sin. Jesus always loves the sinner but hates the sin.
>
> *Lust* is sexual perversion. God created us male and female and instilled in us an attraction toward one another, but lust views the other as an object of self- gratification. Lust distorts the beauty of the sexual act into a fantasy of selfish pleasure.

Greed is pure selfishness and promotes a "me first" attitude. I want it all and I want it now. Greed precludes sharing and promotes hoarding. Jesus renounces greed in the Parable of the Rich Fool (Luke 12: 13-21). Greed is deeply rooted in the material world at the expense of the spiritual one.

Laziness is a waste of the spiritual gifts and talents bestowed by God for His purpose. Satan would much rather have your spiritual gifts lie dormant than for you to use them for God's purpose. Satan loves a couch potato.

Gluttony is excessiveness and lacks moderation. God gave Adam and Eve all of the plants and animals of the world for their food and well- being, but the glutton takes them to the extreme and it becomes a vice. Gluttony does great physical harm to a body which is a temple of the Holy Spirit (1 Cor. 6:19).

Jealousy and envy are cousins. We are jealous of a thing and envious of a person. Jealousy desires a person's house or car or wardrobe or money. We become envious of a person's good looks or intelligence or personality or athletic ability. Jealousy and envy display an unhappiness for who you are and those things that you own. They overlook the unique and special way in which you were created. They imply that God did not do a good enough job when He created you.

Each in its own way, The Seven Deadly Sins are serious offenses which draw us away from the love of God.

Other serious sins which draw us from the love of God include: malice, wishing bad things on another; spite, refusing to share what another person needs; grudge which is rooted in unforgiveness; and ingratitude, resenting another's generosity. These too must be recognized and kept in check.

Satan, however, can have a field day with us by infiltrating our hearts to make us feel as though we are not guilty of any of these offenses when in fact, sometimes we are. He will even have us justify our actions and pervert our hearts to make us believe that we are in the right when we commit these serious offenses. This leads to self-deceit. Self- deceit is the mother of all sin because all sin is born from the thought that we are justified in the evil which we do. It happened first in the Garden of Eden and it continues in our world today. Satan is very good at what he does and we fall prey all too often. Sinful desires which draw us from the love of God must be renounced.

Q 4. Do you turn to Jesus Christ and accept Him as your Savior?

A. *I do.*

The first three questions are questions of renunciation. The final three are questions of acceptance, and this particular question wastes no time in our acceptance of Jesus Christ. This is the most important question of the Baptismal Covenant.

While water is the main symbol of Baptism, "turn" is the main word. The Greek word is "metanoia" which means to turn 180 degrees. This is the essence of Holy Baptism. We turn from our old selves to a new self. *"You were taught, with regard to your former way of life, to put off your old self, which is being corrupted by its deceitful desires; to be made new in the attitude of your minds; and to put on the new self, created to be like God in true righteousness and holiness," (Ephesians*

4:22). This is so linked to the attitude of Christ about which we spoke earlier. It requires that we not only see the world in the way Jesus sees it, but to live Jesus' life in order to put on the lens to do so. Sin must be left at the foot of the cross once and for all. This is no more apparent than the conversion of Paul and his Baptism in The Book of Acts Chapter 9.

If we know that sin is a rebellion against God; if we know that sin alienates us from God and from each other; if we know that sin plays into the devil's hand; if we know that sin causes death; then why do we return to it? It makes no sense. The problem is that we enjoy our sin and we are hesitant to leave it behind. It is a source of pleasure and it is difficult to leave pleasurable things by the wayside. That is the seduction of Satan, and we must turn away from him and toward Jesus.

The point of accepting Jesus Christ as your Savior is the cornerstone of the Baptismal Covenant. It is to turn away from our sinfulness and toward God's grace. It is to turn away from the world and toward the Kingdom. It is to turn way from evil and toward holiness. It is to leave our former selves behind and turn toward a new you. It is to turn 180 degrees. The name Jesus means, "Savior." It is the atoning work of Jesus on the cross by which our sins are paid and we are given the hope of everlasting life. At the crucifixion, the criminal on the right makes such a conversion and he is rewarded with the promise of the Kingdom, but the criminal on the left never makes the turn (Luke 23:39-43).

How often we get things backward. When we find ourselves in a jam, we say, "Lord, help me and then I will serve you." But Jesus says, "No, you serve me first and then I will help you." Jesus raises Lazarus from the dead only after Martha places her faith in Him. Jesus cures Jairus' daughter only after Jairus seeks Him out, and He cures the centurion's servant in like manner. Jesus cures the paralytic after He recognizes the faith of those who lowered him through the roof. The point of conversion is a requirement for Holy Baptism. On the Day of Pentecost when Peter speaks boldly to the crowd about Jesus' death and resurrection, the scriptures tell us, *"Those who accepted his message were baptized, and about three thousand were added to their number that day" (Acts 2:41)*. Acceptance of the message came prior to their Baptism. The only way to Baptism is through the turn; the road of conversion and acceptance.

Q 5. *Do you put your whole trust in his grace and love?*

A. I do.

We have a Border Collie named Dawson who loves to run, run, run. Run, Dawson, run. See Dawson run. Almost daily I strap on my roller blades, put her on her leash, and take her out around the neighborhood just to burn off some of her energy. If we leave the front door or the gate to the back fence open just a crack she will make the most of the opportunity. While we strive to prevent this from happening, she is very quick. When she gets out she can be gone for two hours or two days. It depends on when we receive a phone call announcing her appearance sometimes as many as three miles away.

One Friday afternoon Beth, Anthony and I were planning a trip to Southeast Florida to visit our families. It is about a four hour drive from where we live. When we go out of town we put Dawson in a kennel and we had made arrangements to board her the night before so we could get an early start in the morning. So as I left the Church Office, I stopped for gas at the corner station and my intention was to go home, let

Dawson out in the back yard to do her business and then bring her to the kennel by the 5 pm closing time. Beth and Anthony were not yet home.

Around our back yard I have built a shadow box fence so you cannot see the other side. As I am waiting for the dog, I heard this deep voice from the other side, "Hello?" I responded, "Hello?" The voice continued, "This is Officer Smith from the Clay County Sheriff's Department." My heart skipped a beat. The officer asked, "Did you just purchase gas from the station at Roosevelt and Hibernia?" I responded, "Yes, sir." He continued. "Well, you forgot to pay for it." Defending myself I explained, "Sir, I did pay for it by my debit card." He questioned further, "Do you have a receipt?" I responded, "No sir, the machine was out of paper." The officer explained that someone had pumped gas and drove off without paying and that the girl behind the counter saw my license plate as I was leaving and assumed I was the villain. The officer told me that I would have to follow him back to the gas station to match my card against her register.

All this time we were speaking to each other from opposite sides of the fence and so I opened the gate to speak to him face to face. As I did, guess what? Dawson makes a bee line toward the opening and escapes into freedom. So now I have a police officer ready to escort me to the gas station and a dog on the loose. It is 4 pm. The kennel closes at 5 pm. I explained to the officer that we had plans to go out of town and if I did not find this dog within the next three minutes, she will be gone for days. He told me that he had a couple of minutes to spare.

I ran frantically around our neighborhood looking for her and calling her name, but to no avail. Finally the officer explained that he had no more time and that I would have to follow him now. I raised my hands in the air and out loud I said, "Lord, only you know where this dog is. Please help me find her." Officer Smith chuckled and asked, "Do you expect God to help you find your dog?" With bold confidence, I responded, "Yes, I do." At that moment, a great relief was lifted off of my shoulders and at 4:15 pm I knew that everything was going to work out. If I am not mistaken, I believe I had a smile from ear to ear for Officer Smith.

When we arrived back at the gas station, the lady behind the counter checked my card against her records and realized that I was not the villain and apologized. Apology accepted. Officer Smith then apologized…and accepted. Then he added, "I hope you find your dog." With deep trust, I responded, "I will, with God's help." It was 4:35 pm. The kennel closes at 5 pm.

I drove back to my neighborhood. I said, "OK, God, You know where Dawson is so please point me in the right direction." I drove around asking whomever I saw if they had seen a black and white Border Collie. No takers. It was 4:50 pm. The kennel closes at 5 pm. I made a loop onto which I turned for no apparent reason and there was a crew of carpenters who were breaking for the day. I asked, "Have you seen a black and white Border Collie?" One spoke up and said, "There is a black and white Border Collie who has been sitting by the front of my truck for the past 10 minutes. Now mind you, Dawson loves to run, run, run. So I drove to the front of the carpenter's truck and there is Dawson, just sitting there. She had this look like, "Where in the heck have you been?" So I opened up the door of my truck and I said, "Come on, girl." And she flew in and we were off. It was 4:55 pm. The kennel closes at 5 pm.

I can't say I maintained legal speed on the way to the kennel, but when I arrived, the girl who was closing just happened to be delayed because another customer was picking up his dog. She graciously took Dawson to the back room where she would spend the next few days. It was 5:10 and every-thing was fine. Do I trust God?....Do you have to ask?

A simple story about a boy and his dog; simple trust in the Lord God. Trust is essential in any relationship. If you have already placed *"...your whole trust in His grace and love"* then you are shaking your head in agreement because you understand. Perhaps you have had a similar experience. If you have not yet placed your whole trust in Him then you probably need more proof. But proof is not trust. In The New Testament of the word "faith" is more closely associated with the word "trust" than it is with the word, "believe" (3). In other words, to have faith means that you have trust.

The story about Dawson is one of a hundred stories I could relay to you about times when I have placed all of my trust in Him. When you do it once, you will begin to look for opportunities to trust more and more. God is not so busy that He is apathetic toward even my simple concerns, like getting my dog to the kennel. God is a personal God. He handles the problems of everyone in the world, but He also handles my problems. How He does it I do not know. But He is God. He can handle it.

Would the world have ended if I did not make it to the kennel on time? No, of course not! We would have just delayed our trip for an hour or so the next morning until the kennel opened. No big deal. But we did not have to use Plan B because there was so much trust in Plan A. In fact, I can honestly say that there was so much trust at the time that I did not even think of Plan B. Spending time to consider a Plan B would have eroded the trust I knew I should have in Plan A. When I told Officer Smith that God was going to help me find my dog, that weight was lifted off of my shoulders. I could feel it. Long before it happened, I knew it was going to work out. If I had not prayed, would the girl at the kennel been there after hours checking out another dog? I do not believe so, but that is a moot point. All I know is that I prayed and I trusted and things worked out. That's enough for me. It's enough to take me to the next level of trust.

If I can have so much trust in God with the little things, then I don't feel like such a stranger when I go to Him with the big things. And if I am confident that God will take care of the little things, then I have a ton of confidence that He will take care of the big things. Trust breeds trust. God is a personal God. The important thing is not being afraid to ask for help. Go to God even in the simplest of things; even those things which you think you can handle yourself. Every time you rely on Him it adds to the relationship and each of those times is a building stone of a solid foundation. So let me ask, *"Do you put your whole trust in His grace and love?"*

Q 6. *Do you promise to follow Him as your Lord?*

A. *I do.*

"For Christ did not enter a sanctuary made by human hands, a true copy of the true one, but he entered into heaven itself, now to appear in the presence of God on our behalf. Nor was it to offer Himself again and again, as the High Priest enters the holy place year after year with blood that is not his own; for then he would have to suffer again and again since the foundation of the world. But as it is, he has appeared once for all at the end of the age to remove sin by the sacrifice of himself," (Hebrews 9: 24-26).

"All glory be to Thee, Almighty God, our Heavenly Father, for that Thou, of Thy tender mercy, didst give Thine only Son Jesus Christ to suffer death upon the cross for our redemption; Who made there, by His one oblation once offered, a full, perfect, and sufficient sacrifice, oblation, and satisfaction, for the sins of the whole world," (Eucharistic Prayer I; Rite One; BCP, 334).

Jesus Christ is the Savior of the world. The passage from Hebrews explains that Jesus had to suffer and die only once for the sins of the world and the beautiful words from our Rite One Service proclaims that Jesus' death is sufficient for all sins. These passages proclaim to us that Jesus' atoning work on the cross pays in full the price of the sins of the world; not just those sins which were committed prior to the crucifixion, but for every sin after as well. There is no wiggle room here. There is no sin left unaccounted for. Jesus Christ is your personal Savior. This means that Jesus died for the sins of everyone in the world, but He also died for your sins... everyone of them. There is no sin you have committed or any sin any human who has walked or ever will walk on the face of the earth could commit that has not been paid for by the cross of Jesus Christ. From every mass murder to every white lie, Jesus Christ, the Son of God has picked up the tab through His blood on the cross. "Yea but, what about the time..." Forget it. It's paid for.

Only two questions remain: Why then do you harbor a grudge through your inability to forgive someone who has offended you? And, why can't you forgive yourself for sins and mistakes you have made in the past? By doing so, are you not suggesting that Jesus' death was insufficient? Are you not suggesting that Jesus died for all sins except the ones that you have committed and those who have sinned against you? Are they not covered in the Almighty Plan for Salvation? If Jesus can forgive those who were nailing Him to the cross, surely you can grant forgiveness. You must forgive. You are commanded to forgive. It is part of Jesus' command to us to love one another (John 15:12). Jesus Christ is the Savior of the world.

Many people accept Jesus as their Savior, but not as their Lord. A lord rules your life. He has authority over you. You are his servant. To accept Jesus as your Savior but not as your Lord is the pit of hypocrisy. It means that you are willing to accept what He can do for you, but unwilling to consider what you can do for Him. Reread Bonheoffer's chapter on *Cheap and Costly Grace*. To turn to Jesus is total change; any sin is unacceptable. The Baptismal Covenant into which we enter must totally transform our lives. Baptism is present tense.

When a person does accept Jesus as both Lord and Savior, then powerful things begin to happen. A spiritual awakening propels the individual into an entirely new way of living. Baptism becomes a mile marker on the spiritual journey that distinguishes between the former life and the new one.

This is so remarkably demonstrated in the life of Paul. Once he was baptized by Ananias, an absolute and total change came over him. He went from being a murderer of Christians to one of our most powerful saints. Even the disciples were initially skeptical. It wasn't until the disciple Barnabas explained to the rest that he had heard Paul speak fearlessly in the name of Jesus did they believe (Acts 9:26-29). When a person does accept Jesus as Lord AND Savior, he/she opens the door to God's grace and promises.

Faith is like a bicycle built for two. While steering and peddling our way through life, we take great comfort knowing that Jesus is on the back seat giving us support. But the moment of faith comes when we stop the bike, get off, and change places allowing Jesus to take us where He wants to go. That is the moment of faith. That is the moment of truth.

I was once counseling a 32 year old woman who was married at age 19 and divorced at 21. The divorce had put her on a path which eventually led her to the Lord slowly and gradually, over the course of many years. She was a member of my parish and she would come in every once in a while for a spiritual check- up much like you would have a physical checkup with your doctor. It was evident that she had reached the moment of faith. It was evident by what she said and how she said it. It is not always easy to tell that someone has truly found Jesus. Some people talk the talk, but do not walk the walk. A person who has met the Lord will be doing both. Remember, it was what Paul said and did that convinced Barnabas that Paul was for real. This young woman was for real.

This woman told me that she had completely handed over her entire life to the Lord. She explained that she does not make a move without Almighty consultation. She told me, "I tried to run my life on my own and I messed it up. I have come to realize that I need help. I have turned everything over to Jesus because He knows better." She was on the right track. After her divorce, she prayed and prayed that the Lord would lead her to meet someone of whom He approved and who would make a suitable spouse. She found that person and they have been happily married ever since. You see, the man she met had been praying the same prayer.

Unfortunately, it sometimes takes a disaster like a divorce to bring someone to accept Jesus as Lord. I would dare to say that this is true in the vast majority of cases; that those who have accepted Jesus as their Lord have done so through a crises. It is only then do we realize our complete dependence on Him. It is only then do we realize that He knows better. Crises are opportunities to grow in the faith, to get off of the bike and change seats.

The truth is that we want to be in control. We want things our way. We want to lead, not follow. Once again, however, the Gospel turns us around. Remember that the main word in Baptism is "turn." "Do you turn to Jesus Christ and accept Him as your Savior?" We hand things over but we quickly take them back. We think that God isn't listening or that we can do a better job. We follow until it becomes uncomfortable. We are a servant until we are asked to do too much. Dietrich is rolling over in his grave. "Cheap grace!" he would proclaim. Your attitude must be like Jesus; a humble servant obedient unto death.

So how do you hand anything over much less your entire life? How do you follow Jesus as your Lord? The key reverts back to trust. Trust that Jesus is on top of things, that He wants to help you and knows the best answer. You MUST move away from the attitude that Jesus and the Father are too busy for you. You must fully trust that God is a personal God and that Jesus is your personal Savior. To think differently is nothing but Satan whispering in your ear. Baptism is present tense because Jesus is present tense…24/7. Why would the One Who created you or the One Who died for you or the One Who anoints you not have time for you? You're joking…right?

But you must be willing to follow. You must allow Him to lead even when the road ahead isn't very clear. If in your prayer, you have given Jesus permission to lead your life and the road ahead does not look too appealing, you must not back down. Those times are opportunities to trust. If you are truly following Him then you must brace yourself for any-thing and everything. You must understand that during these times Satan will work on you big time. He will tell you to quit, to take things over, to go back to running things your-self. But don't. Doing so will only invite more disaster. Doing so will put you back to square one. Push on. I give to you the acronym, "P.U.S.H." Pray Until Something Happens. The end will be very rewarding. If you are truly following Jesus, what do you have to lose? *Do you promise to follow Him as your Lord?* Today…this moment…make that promise to Him.

Tough Questions

We just went through six very tough questions. But remember our purpose when we set out; to show what Baptism is and what it is not. It is NOT just a nice ceremony or an enrollment into some Eternal Insurance Policy. It IS a cove-nant, a spiritual agreement. It is more serious than most people imagine. But it is also and most importantly, a relationship; a relationship built on trust and acceptance, obedience and com-mitment, and a rejection of everything else that gets in the way. In our next section, we will talk about this relationship. If you understand the nature of each of these questions and if you agree with the way each should be properly answered, then you have a solid understanding of Holy Baptism and are able to move away from many of its myths and misunderstandings.

Questions

1. The Church is trying to dispel some of the myths associ-ated with Baptism. What myths regarding Baptism have you previously held?

2. Some opponents of the Episcopal Church contend that our theology is watered down and they even go so far as to say that we are, "Catholic-lite." How would you respond to their argument considering the vows that are required at Baptism?

3. Would it be going too far to require a Candidate for Holy Baptism to read Dietrich Bonhoffer's, **The Cost of Discipleship** in its entirety?

4. Which of the six Baptismal questions is most difficult for you to answer?

5. When did you, "…turn to Jesus Christ and accept Him as your Savior?"

6. I related a story about my dog in which I placed total trust in the Spirit's ability to help me find her. Can you also give witness to an event in which you placed total trust in God?

7. Faith is like a bicycle built for two. Are you able to stop the bicycle of your life and allow Jesus to steer?

Section IV:

Spirit of Adoption

" For you did not receive a spirit that makes you a slave again to fear, but you received a spirit of adoption. And by him we cry, 'Abba, Father.' The Spirit himself testifies with our spirit that we are God's children" (Rom. 8:15,16).

*L*ike many pets, we adopted our Border Collie, Dawson from a Safe Animal Shelter. My wife and I grew up in homes that always had pet dogs and we know what a joy they can be, but also a lot of responsibility. For this reason even though our son had been begging for a dog for a couple of years, my wife and I kept postponing the decision. Finally on his sixth birthday, Beth and I decided that the time was right.

The three of us went to an Animal Shelter. There were a lot of dogs from which to choose, but none of them felt like the right mix. We were just about ready to leave when the woman who ran the shelter asked us to wait a few more minutes. "There is one more dog I want you to see." She came out from the back with this most precious dog, a Border Collie. "Her name is Dawson," said the woman. Our son and the dog bonded immediately and without further questions, we knew she was the one for us. We signed the papers and adopted her. She became our dog.

I loved Dawson from the very beginning not only because our son loved her, but I quickly developed a genuine affection for her. I knew she was going to be in the family a long time and after all, she had been abandoned and relegated to an animal shelter. She touched my heart immediately and by the time we arrived home, I felt that the four of us were beginning to bond as a family.

We soon discovered, however, that Dawson had problems with me. She really kept her distance. She was actually afraid of me. This went on for quite a while. Beth and I concluded that she must have been abused by a man. How anyone could have abused this innocent creature of God was beyond us, but that was the only reason that made sense. We concluded that Dawson had a genuine fear of men.

One evening, however, while the three of us were playing with her, Dawson came over, jumped up on my lap and gave me a big tongue lapping kiss. We were all amazed! It made me feel so good! In her own little way she overcame her fear, broke down the barriers between us and reciprocated the love that I had been pouring her way. I gave her a big hug and she threw more kisses my way. I felt as though I had finally gotten through to her. I was not the demon from her past. In my mind, at that moment, the adoption became official. *"For you did not receive a spirit that makes you a slave again to fear, but you have received a spirit of adoption."*

Dawson and I are now best buds. A vet once told me that the memory of a dog lasts about six months so her memories of an abused past are long gone. She has a good home now; a safe home filled with love and joy, and there are times when her tail wags so voraciously that it looks like it's about to fall off.

Baptism is much the same. God created each of us and yearns to form a strong bond of incredible love from the very beginning. Psalm 139 prays,

> *"For you created my inmost parts;*
> *you knit me together in my mother's womb" (vs.12).*

God loved us from the very beginning; while we were being fashioned in the womb. In fact, He put each of us together. And God has showered us with incredible blessings and has sent many incredible things our way. But for some reason we keep our distance; perhaps a demon from the past which prevents us from responding to God's call. A dog's memory lasts six months, but unfortunately human memory can last years, even decades. We become lost and disorientated. We want to, but we are afraid. The moment of Baptism, however, is the moment we break down the barriers and reciprocate the love with which God has showered our lives. It is the moment we jump up on God's lap and give Him a big hug. That is the moment of Baptism. That is the moment that the adoption becomes official.

My wife and I are very good friends with a couple who began attending our Church and eventually became members. This made the relationship a little different because usually a clergy couple becomes friends with people who are already parishioners; priest first, friends later. Our relationship with these friends evolved in the opposite way; friends first, priest later. The couple is several years younger than we are and when we first met them, they were struggling to have children. Tests revealed only a slight possibility of this happening, the topic of conversations the four of us had on a couple of occasions. In fact, these conversations were partially influential in leading them to our Church as we read and discussed the stories of Abraham and Sarah, and Elizabeth and Zechariah, and even though these forerunners of our faith were beyond childbearing years, we were convinced that God had something up His Almighty sleeve.

As time passed and still no pregnancy, the couple eventually began considering alternate methods of parenthood. After much prayer, soul searching and ruling out other options, they decided to investigate the possibility of adopting a child. They were given the name of a lawyer two hours away who specialized in the adoption of children yet unborn and they made an appointment just to ask some questions (about a hundred if I remember correctly). Beth and I knew about the appointment and we joined them in prayer, but we were not prepared for what was about to take place.

The appointment was for 10 am. At 11 am, I was sitting in my office when they called from a park bench. After answering only half of their questions, the lawyer informed them of three case scenarios of pregnant women with whom he was presently working and that there was another couple coming later that afternoon and they would certainly choose one of them. Our friends called for further prayer and spiritual direction. Helping to clarify the gamut of their emotions, I thought there were only two fundamental questions; "Is God calling you to adopt a child now?" If the answer to that question is "No," then get in your car and head home. If the answer to that question is "Yes," then which child do you choose? I encouraged them to allow God to make that decision as well and not to decide solely on whether they wanted a son or a daughter. An hour later, they returned to the lawyer's office confident that this is where God was leading them and they proceeded with the legal process with a pregnancy too early to tell the sex of their unborn child. Months later they became the proud parents of a little baby girl.

Living through that experience with them, I can tell you that adoption leaves you extremely vulnerable. It is such a spiritual, emotional, and financial commitment. Their trust in God was essential. But their joy was incredible.

The adoption process is deeply spiritual. Parents of adopted children have the unique advantage of "choosing" the time, the situation, and the child. Baptism is much the same. Jesus tells us, *"You did not choose me, but I chose you and appointed you to go and bear fruit-fruit that will last. Then the Father will give you whatever you ask in my name. This is my command: Love one another" (John 15: 16,17).* Adoption is love.

Their adopted daughter bears their name, is part of their family, receives their love, and one day will inherit their fortune. In like manner, at Baptism we are adopted into God's family, receive His tremendous love, share His life, and will inherit the Kingdom. I can think of no greater analogy to describe this Holy Sacrament than that of adoption. Baptism is adoption. Adoption is love. Baptism is reciprocated love. "Holy Baptism is the sacrament by which God adopts us as His children and makes us members of Christ's Body, the Church, and inheritors of the Kingdom of God" (**Book of Common Prayer,** 858).

But if God created us and formed us in the womb, then why is adoption necessary? Are we not already His children and is He not already Our Father? Did Jesus not die for the unbaptized as well? To answer these questions, we must better understand this whole notion of reciprocated love. If we had not adopted Dawson, would she have remained alive? Yes. Would she have been adopted by someone else? Possibly/probably. But she would not have been *our* pet. If our friends had not adopted their daughter would she have been adopted by another couple? Yes. But she would not have been *their* daughter; as Mommy puts it, "A match made in heaven." Baptism is about a relationship of reciprocated love by Someone Who has chosen you and Whom you eventually have chosen.

A "Baptism of adoption" is also necessary because of the world of sin. God created each of us, "formed us in the womb," but this relationship suffered alienation through human sin. Sin alienates us from God, drives a wedge into the very heart of our relationship with Him. Through sin, there is formed a gap between each person and our Creator.

This gap is very evident in the Parable of the Prodigal Son (Luke 15: 11-32). The younger son who took his share of the inheritance traveled to a land far away (the gap) where he squandered his money in dissolute living (the sin). The scriptures are outstanding at this point because the turning point of the story is verse 17 which opens, *"But when he came to himself..."*

When he came to himself! What an awesome description! When he came to understand that he could not make it on his own. When he came to understand that there was a gap between him and his father. When he came to realize how grievously he had sinned. When he came to understand that there was also a gap between him and himself. *"When he came to himself..."* That is the point when he begins to make his way back to his father who waits with open arms. And when he finally makes his way home, the reciprocated love leads to an embrace. That is the moment of Baptism. The relationship would never be the same.

Did the prodigal ever lose his status of being his father's son? No. Did the father ever give up on his son? No! Was the father heart- broken because of his son's actions? Yes! But how glorious the reunion. The sin was repented. The gap was filled. The celebration began. I believe the celebratory meal that the father gives in the Parable of the Prodigal Son is the closest example in scripture of a reception following a Baptism.

"And by Him we cry, 'Abba, Father.'" But "Abba" is intended to be more personal, more intimate. It truly means, "Daddy" (1). What child runs around the house using the formal term "father?" Kids say, "Dad," or "Daddy." This is the way God wants us to address Him. That is the type of relationship for which God yearns to have with us. The word, "father" implies respect, yes, but also some distance. Respect from fear? We are called to the opposite. We are called out of fear. We are called to a spirit of adoption.

If we had adopted Dawson and she remained fearful of men, then her love for me would have never developed. And even though I had an immediate affection for her, it was only when her memory left the past behind that her love for me became complete. If our friends had adopted their daughter and she refused their love and became indifferent toward them, then even though they would not have loved her less and the adoption would still have been legal, it would never have been fulfilled. Their relationship with their daughter is made complete through her relationship with them.

In like manner, we are able to love because God loved us first (1 John 4:18). But a relationship is not formed until God's love is reciprocated. Otherwise it remains a one way street. Reciprocated love is the essence of any relationship and while God loves us from the beginning, a relationship with God is not made complete until we are baptized. Baptism is our spiritual birth. Jesus explains to Nicodemus, *"I tell you the truth, no one can see the Kingdom of God unless he is born again. No one can enter the Kingdom of God unless he is born of water and the Spirit. Flesh gives birth to flesh, but the Spirit gives birth to spirit. You must not be surprised at my saying, 'You must be born again'" (John 3: 3, 5-7).*

Baptism is all about forming a relationship of reciprocated love with the One Who created you by being reborn in the spirit of adoption. It is about jumping up on God's lap and giving Him a tongue lapping kiss. It is about responding to Jesus because He has chosen you. It is about becoming a reflection of the image of God with which you were created. It is about becoming a member of God's family and looking forward to the Kingdom. *"The Spirit himself testifies with our spirit that we are God's children" (Romans 8:17).*

Holy Communion

"All baptized Christians following the Lord Christ are welcome to receive Holy Communion,"

(…words of the celebrant at Trinity Episcopal Church, St. Augustine following The Invitation to Communion).

"I am the bread of life. Whoever comes to me will never be hungry, and whoever believes in me will never be thirsty. Your ancestors ate manna in the desert and they died. This is the bread which comes from heaven, so that one may eat

of it and not die. I am the living bread that came down from heaven. Whoever eats of this bread will live forever; and the bread that I will give for the life of the world is my flesh,"
(John 6: 35, 49-51).

In the Episcopal Church, Holy Baptism gives a person the privilege of receiving Holy Communion. According to the Canons of the Church and the rubrics of The Prayer Book, a person must be baptized before they are allowed to receive the Body and Blood of Jesus Christ. Holy Baptism and Holy Communion are called *The Sacraments of Initiation* because they are the introduction of a sacramental life for the individual and they are the two sacraments instituted by Jesus in the Gospels. Receiving Holy Communion brings intimacy into our relationship with Jesus Christ. We are made one with Him by receiving His Body and Blood.

In the Episcopal Church, we believe in the Real Presence of Jesus Christ in Holy Communion. We believe that He is truly present in the bread and truly present in the wine. We are not sure how this happens, but we accept it by faith (2). For us, Holy Communion is not a symbol. The words of Jesus at The Last Supper were, *"This IS my Body. This IS my Blood."* Jesus did not say, *"This represents my Body,"* or *"This is a symbol of my Blood."* We believe in the real thing. We believe in the real deal. We believe in the Real Presence.

If you could see what happens to you when you receive Holy Communion you would be blown away. If you could put on a pair of spiritual 3D glasses so that you could see the spiritual world as you consume the Body and Blood of Jesus Christ, you would never want to leave the Church. The term, "Communion of the Saints" would take on a whole new meaning. And as the Eucharist is directly connected to the

Last Supper which was a celebration of the Passover Meal, I believe you would also meet some of our ancestors from 3500 years ago.

For this reason, when my wife and I moved into the Episcopal Church, I had a difficult time allowing our then two year old son, Anthony to take Communion. I did not think he should receive Holy Communion until he was a little older and better understood what was going on, so when we went up to the rail, I would always make sure his arms were folded and he would just receive a blessing. I thought that when he turned 6 or 7 years old, I could explain things to him and at least he would have some idea of what was going on.

One Sunday in an act of independence, Anthony stuck out his hands as the priest came by distributing the bread. It was very quick. All in one motion he held out his hands in perfect form, the priest placed the bread in his tiny hands and he ate it before dad had time to blink. I could not believe what I had just seen. I must have had a terrified look on my face because the priest, who was a good friend of mine, just chuckled. "Was this prearranged?" I thought. Could this toddler son of ours be part of a great conspiracy? Did our son and the priest need The Reconciliation of a Penitent? I pulled his hands back just in time as the Chalice Bearer carrying the consecrated wine arrived.

After the service the priest asked me why I was displeased with our son's actions. I told him that Anthony really didn't understand what he was doing. He asked, "Does your son understand the digestive system of the body?" I responded, "Of course not." He replied, "Then do you withhold food from him?" OK...I thought. That made sense. He needs the food whether he understands it or not. The priest continued, "Just because your son does not understand what the Eucharist is all about, that does not invalidate the sacrament. It is still the Body and the Blood of Christ and you son needs the spiritual food. That is not diminished once ounce by a lack of understanding." He definitely gave me something about which to think.

The more I thought about it, the analogy made more and more sense. And so when we arrived back home, I sat Anthony on a chair and I asked him, "Son, what did you do today in Church?" He said, "I ate the bread." I asked, "What is the bread?" He responded, "The bread is Jesus."

I was so moved by that simple conversation. Looking back, it has been one of the most memorable conversations with our son I have ever had. Could it be that for weeks, perhaps even months our son had been longing to receive Holy Communion knowing that it was Jesus and had not been able to because his blind and narrow minded father would not allow him? Could it be that he had to quickly sneak it before his dad stopped the entire thing? Could the chuckle of the priest been that of Jesus, Himself? I looked into our son's deep brown eyes and felt the reciprocated love that was being transferred back and forth. The relationship that I had with my son had just moved to the next level. It included my son's relationship with Jesus. "From now on," I explained to him, "Every time we go to Church, you can take the bread as long as you remember it's Jesus." It goes without saying, our son has received Holy Communion every Sunday since.

"Then little children were being brought to him in order that he might lay his hands on them and pray. The disciples spoke sternly to those who brought them; but Jesus said, 'Let the little children come to me, and do not stop them; for it is to such as these that the kingdom of heaven belongs,"
(Matt. 19: 13,14).

For baptized adults who have a little better understanding, the Eucharist provides an intimacy not attainable in human relationships. When you receive Holy Communion, you consume the Body and the Blood of Jesus Christ. He comes into your heart and soul. He lives in your body which is the temple of the Holy Spirit (1 Cor. 6:19) and from there He offers sacrifices to the Father. Put on the spiritual 3D glasses and observe what takes place. Human songs which long for closer intimacy between the lovers cannot hold a candle to the intimacy achieved with our Lord and Savior through Holy Communion.

Unfortunately, some adults do not see the necessity of going to Church and receiving Holy Communion. They say, "I can pray to God on the golf course, or when I am out fishing, or when I am at the beach." And this is all true and hopefully they are indeed praying during these times. But they will not find a worshipping community in these locations nor can they avail themselves to the Body and the Blood of Jesus Christ. What He has to offer is far better than a birdie, a five pound bass, or the perfect wave on which to surf. And please, don't even mention rolling over and to get more sleep.

The last thing Satan wants is for you to become intimate with our Lord and Savior. He will fill you with any excuse to pass up an opportunity to become one with God through His Son. He will even make you feel guilty enough to make you think you do not deserve it. However, it is precisely those times when you need it the most. Jesus tells us, *"I have come only for the lost sheep of Israel," (Mt. 15:24)*. There are so many instances in the Gospels where Jesus eats with sinners. He is in the midst of them and shares a meal; breaks bread with them. These meals with sinners point to the Eucharist and our sharing a meal with Him; Jesus every week. Don't deny yourself the soul food for which your soul longs. Baptism gives you the privilege of receiving Holy Communion. Don't miss out.

As we adopted Dawson into our family, through your Baptism, God adopts you into His family. God has chosen you at this place and time in your life. He has hand-picked you to be with Him. You will bear His name as a Christian. You will share in His life. You will inherit His Kingdom. You will be able to become one with Him through Holy Communion. God is calling you. It is a wonderful thing that you plan to respond.

Questions

1. Have you ever adopted a pet? If so, compare that experience to being adopted into God's Family at Baptism.
2. Pray Psalm 139 in its entirety. Do you feel special?
3. Adoption is love. Is the thought of being adopted by God and one day inheriting the Kingdom the source of true joy in your life?
4. The turning point in The Parable of the Prodigal Son is when the son, "… came to himself." Describe a time in your sin that you came to yourself which led you to the road of repentance.
5. In the Episcopal Church, Baptism gives us the privilege of receiving Holy Communion. Do you understand what is meant by The Real Presence?
6. Do you allow your baptized children to receive Holy Communion? Why/Why not?
7. What excuses keep you from going to Church every Sunday and receiving Jesus every week?

Section V:

The Baptism of Jesus and Life in the Spirit

"Then Jesus came from Galilee to be baptized by John. But John tried to deter him saying, 'I need to be baptized by you, and do you come to me?' Jesus replied, 'Let it be so now; it is proper for us to do this to fulfill all righteousness.' Then John consented.

As soon as Jesus was baptized, he went up out of the water. At that moment heaven was opened, and he saw the Spirit of God descending like a dove and lighting on him. And a voice from heaven said, 'This is my Son, whom I love; with him I am well pleased'" (Matthew 3: 13-17).

This passage gives two reasons as to why Jesus had to be baptized: 1) for the fulfillment of righteousness, and 2) for the indwelling of the Holy Spirit. Let us set out to discover what each of these mean.

The Fulfillment of Righteousness

Humans were created in the image of God, made from God's love to share in His life. Love is designed to be given away. The natural flow of love is outward, away from yourself. Like gravity that pulls everything down, love pushes everything away. Any love that you keep for yourself becomes selfish and perverted, like keeping something in the refrigerator too long; it becomes moldy and mildewed. And so God had all of this love and He longed to give it away; so He created humans. Humans were created to be the recipients of God's divine love and the fact that there have been so many of us in the course of human history gives us an insight into vastness of God's eternal love. God longs to love us and He longs for us to love Him. That was the original design of creation.

Further, I personally believe that the earth was originally designed to be an extension of heaven, sort of like a satellite of a university in another city. God's original vision for the earth was much different than the present reality. When God fashioned the universe, He did so with the intention of all of us loving one another, living in harmony with nature, with each other, and in unity with Him. God's original plan of creation was based on a divine vision of incredible love that is beyond our wildest imagination.

"What is man that you should be mindful of him?
The son of man that you should seek him out?
You have made him but little lower than the angels;
You adorn him with glory and honor;
You give him mastery over the works of your hands;
You put all things under his feet:
All sheep and oxen,

> *Even the wild beasts of the field,*
> *The birds of the air, the fish of the sea,*
> *And whatsoever walks in the paths of the sea.*
> *O Lord our Governor,*
> *How exalted is your name in all the world!"*

(Psalm 8: 5-10).

William Temple, Archbishop of Canterbury during the early 1920's believed that when God created the world He had already decided to send His Son to earth just to show us how much He loves us. Temple believed that the original mission of the Son of God was solely to be an ambassador of the Father's incredible love. The Son's only purpose in coming to earth was to assure us humans how much the Father loves us (1).

You can almost imagine a conversation taking place at the very dawn of creation between the Father and the Son. After everything had been created, the Father turns to the Son and says, "One day when the time is right, I want you to go to earth as one of them and just tell them over and over and over again how much I love them. I want them to be absolutely convinced of my love for them. You have got to make it very clear beyond a shadow of a doubt that I will love them forever." And the Son in absolute obedience replies, "That is an excellent idea, Father. I will be honored to do that for You. You just tell me when."

All of this changed through the sin of Adam. Adam's sin tainted God's original design. The earth as heaven's university satellite lost its accreditation and humankind was alienated from our intimacy with our Creator. God's incredible love for humanity had a wedge driven into it. God's vision had been lost. And it didn't take very long at all for this to happen. Humans are created in Genesis Chapter One, but by Genesis Chapter Three we had already sinned.

Something had to be done. The earth had to be recreated and humans had to be reconciled. God was not about to give up on us. He had too much of His love invested in us. The human race needed a new beginning. Because of Adam's sin, God had to redesign creation. Sin forced God into Plan B. Archbishop Temple believed at the time of Adam's sin, the mission of the Son on earth changed to include His sacrificial death to atone for our sinfulness (2).

You can almost imagine a second conversation taking place between the Father and the Son after Adam's fall. The Father says to the Son, "Because of human sin, your mission has to be updated. Not only must you tell them how much I love them, but you must bear the weight of their sin upon your own shoulders so that their *righteousness may be restored*. Otherwise, they will have no way of entering our Kingdom. Your death will also be a further testimony of my incredible for love for them and will restore all of humanity into the perfect peace of our love. Then when you rise from the dead, they will be given the hope of eternal life with us in the Kingdom." And again in perfect obedience, the Son replies, "I understand what must be done, Father. I will be honored to do that for you. You just tell me when." As Paul explains in Philippians 2; *"And being found in human form, he humbled himself and became obedient to the point of death-even death on a cross," (vs. 6).*

Eucharistic Prayer A, Rite II of our Episcopal Liturgy prays:

"Holy and Gracious Father: in Your infinite love you made us for yourself; and when we had fallen into sin and become subject to evil and death, you, in your mercy, sent Jesus

*Christ, your only and eternal Son, to share our human
nature, to live and die as one of us, to reconcile us to You,
the God and Father of all"* (**Book of Common Prayer,** 362).

I once had a conversation with a parishioner who struggled to understand Jesus' mission on earth. She viewed Jesus'
mission solely as fatalistic; "The Son of God was born to
die." She had a difficult time understanding why God would
allow this to happen. It simply did not make sense to her. But
Archbishop Temple presents a very different point of view.
According to Archbishop Temple, the Son of God became
human primarily out of the Father's love. The plan for His
sacrifice came later. The Father's plan for His Son was not
originally fatalistic, but one of deep, deep love. In fact, the
willingness of the Father to sacrifice His Son is a testimony to
the love that the Father has for us.

I tell my congregation that they should thank their lucky
stars that I am not God because I would not be willing to sacrifice my only son for them. It is not out of a lack of love for
them, but because I love my son too much. I would not be able
to watch my son go through what the Father watched His Son
go through.

It is amazing to think that before the Son of God left
heaven to become one of us, He knew what was in store; the
rejection He was to experience and the death He was to suffer.
He was aware that He would become unaware; that He would
share even in our ignorance. And yet because of His complete
obedience to His Father, He accepted the mission anyway. As
the voice from the heaves proclaims, *"This is my Son, whom I
love; in him I am well pleased."*

It is also amazing to think that before the Son of God left
heaven to come to earth as one of us, He worked with the

Father and the Holy Spirit to create His own mother, Mary. Imagine that! Creating your own mother. What would you change about her? Mary, the mother of God; She talks to angels. They call her out by her name (cf: Luke 1: 26-38). Did I tell you that He has His mother's eyes?

As the Father recreates the world spiritually through His Son, Jesus becomes the Second Adam. *"For since death came through a man, the resurrection of the dead comes also through a man. For as in Adam all die, so in Christ all will be made alive"* (1 Corinthians 15: 21, 22). And again; *"So it is written: 'The first man Adam became a living being,' the last Adam, a life giving spirit"* (1 Corinthians 15: 45).

It was through Adam's sin that the body and the soul began fighting with each other. As mentioned previously, everything in the Old Testament is fulfilled in the New Testament. This theme of fulfillment dominates the scriptures. Everything in the Old Testament points to the coming of the Son of God at Christmas and everything in the New Testament is the result of this fulfillment and points to the Kingdom. Jesus, the Second Adam is the fulfillment of the first Adam.

Jesus is the Second Adam, the fulfillment of creation through Whom the righteousness of all of creation is restored. This is the meaning of the first part of Jesus' response to John the Baptist. Jesus had to be baptized because all of humanity had to be baptized and reconciled to the Father. All of humanity is personified in the Son of God, Jesus the Christ. It is for this reason that He is able to become our sacrificial lamb and die for our sins; all of our sins. The role of Jesus not only as the Son of God, but also as the Son of Man begins to evolve because through Jesus, the righteousness of all of humanity is restored. By tapping into Jesus' Baptism at our own Baptism, we share in the infinite love, grace and mercy of the Father.

"In him, you have delivered us from evil, and made us worthy to stand before you. In him, you have brought us out of error into truth, out of sin into righteousness, out of death into life,"

(Holy Eucharist II; Eucharistic Prayer B, **BCP,** 368).

When John the Baptist questions Jesus about His Baptism and Jesus responds, *Let it be so for now; it is proper for us to do this for all righteousness to be restored,"* it is only because John would never have understood the significance of it all. The plot was far from being fully revealed. It was the very beginning of Jesus' public ministry and this part of the History of Salvation would have been unfathomable for John to understand. How much Jesus, Himself understood about His ministry is even widely speculated, but John, in perfect obedience to his Master, consented and Jesus is baptized.

The Indwelling of the Holy Spirit

Jesus lived 33 years. For the first 30 years, He lived in private working with His earthly father, Joseph the carpenter, and observing all of the Jewish traditions. These years are commonly referred to as His private ministry; teaching us to live a life of prayer and fasting, to honor God by obeying the commandments, and to honor and obey your parents. While the scriptures give us little information about this period of His life, He did all things a faithful Jew was expected to do. He was circumcised at eight days old, presented in the temple as the firstborn male, went to the synagogue on the Sabbath, made a pilgrimage with His parents every year to Jerusalem to celebrate the Passover, and observed all of the Jewish feast days. Luke summarizes these years by simply saying, "*And Jesus grew in wisdom and stature, and with favor with God and men*" (Luke 2:52).

When the Son of God lived on earth for 33 years in the Person of Jesus Christ, He was 100% God and 100% human. He was not half and half. One of the doctrines of our faith is that His divinity did not detract from His humanity, nor did His humanity detract from His divinity (3). Children sometimes believe that Jesus had an unfair advantage in school that because He was the Son of God, He knew the answer before the teacher even asked the question. This conclusion is "childish" because that would be an example of His divinity detracting from His humanity. The truth is that Jesus was born ignorant, like us. His education was gradual, like ours. He had to go to school, like we do. He had to study in order to learn. He did His homework and earned grades. He had to eat and sleep, bathe and go to the bathroom. His parents read bedtime stories to Him and when He was a teenager, He even had a curfew! His divinity did not detract from His humanity.

But Jesus was also 100% God and His humanity did not detract from His divinity. He was God's Son, born of the Virgin Mary. The Apostles' and Nicene Creeds proclaim this, and that the Son lived with the Father and the Spirit in the Kingdom prior to coming to earth as a human. When the Angel Gabriel announces to Mary that she has been chosen to be the mother of God, she questions how this could be since she was still a virgin. Gabriel responds, "*The Holy Spirit will come upon you, and the power of the most high will overshadow you. So the holy one to be born will be called the Son of God*" *(Luke 1:35)*. This is one of the most important verses in all of scripture because without the virgin birth, Jesus could not be God's Son. The manger and the cross are God at his best.

Mary's virginity is a doctrine of the faith; it is not an optional belief. Joseph had nothing to do with Jesus' biological birth. The Holy Spirit took one of Mary's eggs, fertilized it, and implanted it in her womb. The Holy Spirit impregnated Mary. Therefore, Jesus was truly God's Son; 100% God's Son. This is announced at His Baptism, *"This is my Son, Whom I love; with Him I am well pleased," (Mt. 3:17).*

You can imagine another conversation taking place at some time during Jesus' childhood between Jesus and His mother as Mary explains to her Son that He did not come about like all the other little children. "What do you mean, Mom?" Jesus asks. Mary responds, "Well, let's just say that you are very special. Even though Joseph is my husband and your earthly father, your real Father is in heaven above." And then Mary ends with the very popular line used by all parents who have reached their ability to explain a certain thing; "It will all make sense to you one day."

This conversation has two premises: the first is Jesus' share in our ignorance as humans. I don't believe that this can be stressed enough. The truth is that He did not have all of the answers anymore than we have all of the answers. Things were revealed gradually. There are volumes written on the consciousness of Jesus and how much He understood who He was and His role as the Messiah, much less the Son of God. Jesus' Baptism was an eye opener for Him as well as for those who witnessed it. He must have wondered, "What does all of this mean?"

The scriptures tell us that immediately after His Baptism, He retreated into the desert for 40 days to fast and to pray. What a time of revelation those days must have been! Questions such as, "Who am I?" and "What does all of this mean?" and "What do I do now?" must have been pondered over and over. And it is just when we are the most confused that Satan's attacks are the strongest; three times the evil one attacks Jesus. The truth is that Jesus depended upon prayer and fasting to light the path ahead of Him. He appears after that 40 day retreat ready to take the next step and He preaches His first sermon, The Sermon on the Mount (Matthew 5 – 7) in which He explains very clearly that His role is to fulfill the law and the prophets. He could not have preached that sermon prior to the desert experience.

The second premise is that all Jewish children referred to God as their Father. The Psalms they prayed as well as the scriptures to which they listened all had this reference, and Jesus was no exception. Jesus considered God as His Father in the same way all the rest of His friends and schoolmates did, but the biological connection explained by His mother was a new unfolding. The episode in the temple when He was twelve years old was a reference to His understanding as a child of God. Jesus' comment, *"Do you not know that I must be about my Father's business?"* (Luke 2:49). This was not far removed from a comment that any Jewish boy could have proclaimed. And I do not intend to downplay the event because it was evident that Jesus was very astute in His understanding of the scriptures, but to assume that He fully understood the events of His life would be to allow His divinity to diminish His humanity. He would not have been 100% human. The scriptures tell us that Jesus was like us in every way but sin (Hebrews 4:15). Unfortunately for Him, ignorance was part of the deal.

Jesus was baptized so that His divinity and His humanity could work more closely together. Most often, the role of the Holy Spirit is incarnational; to bring the spiritual into the temporal. The times when we feel most Spirit-filled are those times when we are a physical shell to the spiritual indwelling. This is what happened to Jesus when He emerged from the water at His Baptism; He was physically present but spiritually filled. The heavens opened and the Spirit descended upon Him...very, very powerful. His private ministry had come to an end and the first steps of His public ministry left footprints on the banks of the Jordan River.

It is important to understand that Jesus needed to be baptized. His Baptism was not simply to serve as an example for us, but more importantly for Jesus, it was necessary in order to stir up the Spirit within Him and to set His life on a course of obedience to His Father. His humanity had to be fused with His divinity and His divinity had to be fused with His humanity. It was through His Baptism that the path He was to follow became clearer to Him. The time to fulfill Salvation History had come. The journey of a thousand miles had just taken its first eternal step, and although Jesus would spend many more nights in prayer and fasting to discern His Father's Will and to further invite the Spirit into His life, this moment was made very clear to Him and being filled with the Holy Spirit, He probably wished it would never have ended.

The same is true in our own Baptism. Being created body and soul, we share in the image of God and there is often a tension between the two; even a battle between the two. This is the core of spiritual warfare. The indwelling of the Holy Spirit received at Baptism is a spiritual awakening which causes our spiritual lives to be stirred and respond to this battle. We need to be baptized to experience this awakening, just as Jesus needed His Baptism to set Him on a path willed by His Father. Baptism releases the Holy Spirit in our lives and opens the door to many powerful encounters with Him in the future which we would have otherwise missed.

The question is not, "How much of Jesus do you have?" Rather, the question is, "How much of you does Jesus have?" The question is not, "What do you get out of a church service knowing Jesus is there?" The question is rather, "What does Jesus get out of a church service knowing you are there?" To walk in the Spirit does not mean that you invite Jesus to walk by your side everywhere you go. Rather, to walk in the Spirit means that you accept Jesus' invitation to walk by His side everywhere He goes. It's all about Jesus. When you accept this truth and conform your life to it, you too, like Jesus as He came out of the water, will have taken the first steps of your Baptism.

Baptism is present tense because we walk in the walk every day. Baptism has a claim on everything we do. We live in the tension of body and spirit every day. We fight the battle of spiritual warfare every day. We must put on the armor of God every day. We must constantly empty ourselves out of ourselves to make room for the Spirit; more of Him and less of me. This is very often hard to do living in a culture that proclaims more of me; I want it all and I want it now. We must constantly strive to live into the righteousness provided for us by the Son of God by sinning less and becoming more and more holy. *"Be perfect, therefore, as your Heavenly Father is perfect," (Matthew 5:48).* Leading a perfect Christian life is impossible in this earthly one, but it needs to be our goal and it must be a goal from which Satan does not take away through frustration and a lack of perseverance.

God is a personal God. What does this mean? It means that God created the entire world, but He also created you. He did not rush to create you. You were not created haphazardly, or by coincidence, or on some almighty assembly line. You were formed in the womb by the Master. You were knitted together by the Lord. You were thought out...planned out...

and brought forth. And Jesus Christ is your personal Savior. What does this mean? It means that Jesus Christ died for all of the sins of the world, but He also died for your sins; everyone one of them. The Son of God had you on His mind when He came out of the Jordan River and when He was carrying His cross; and He cannot wait for you to meet Him face to face in the Kingdom. Just something to look forward to.

Questions

1. I believe that the earth was originally designed to be an extension of heaven, sort of like a satellite of a university in another city. Do you believe this way as well? Why/ Why not?

2. I imagine two pertinent conversations between the Father and the Son: in the first one, the Father tells the Son to go to the earth as an ambassador of His love; in the second one, the Father tells the Son that while He is down there He will have to take care of our sin. Can you envision other pertinent conversations between the two?

3. The Fulfillment of Righteousness is the atoning work of Jesus on the cross for our sins. Jesus accepted this mission willingly out of love and obedience to His Father. What difficult task has the faith demanded of you and how did you respond?

4. Do you harbor the guilt of sins that you do not think Jesus' death was able to forgive? If so, are you not implying that Jesus' death was not sufficient?

5. A doctrine of our faith is that Jesus' humanity did not detract from His divinity and that His divinity did not detract from His humanity. Have you ever confused this distinction?

6. Describe your most incredible encounter with the Holy Spirit.
7. Jesus completely depended upon the Holy Spirit to give direction to His life and ministry. How often do you go to the Spirit with questions of self- identity, purpose, mission, and decision making?

Section VI:

Gifts of the Holy Spirit

"Now there are a variety of gifts, but the same Spirit; and there are a variety of services, but the same Lord; and there are varieties of activities, but it is the same God who activates all of them in everyone. Now to each one the manifestation of the Spirit is given for the common good," (1 Corinthians 12: 4-7).

"Now you are the body of Christ and individually members of it. And God has appointed in the church first apostles, second prophets, third teachers; then deeds of power, then gifts of healing, forms of assistance, forms of leadership, various kinds of tongues. Are all apostles? Are all prophets? Are all teachers? Do all work miracles? Do all possess gifts of healing? Do all speak in tongues? Do all interpret? But strive for the greater gifts. And I will show you a still more excellent way," (1 Corinthians 12: 27-31).

his is our turn in Salvation History. It is our turn. Each era of this history has played its part in God's Almighty Plan for our redemption and eventual reunion with Him. The Kingdom has been revealed and has been dependent upon the response of certain individuals and people of their day. Abraham did his part, and so did Moses. Without them, the Promised Land of Canaan would not have been realized through the original covenant, the Passover, the desert journey and the expulsion of pagan cultures. The construction of the City of Jerusalem, the reigns of Jesse, David and Solomon, and building the temple, wars, exiles and remnants, and the age of the great prophets all had their turn and played their part. The birth of the Messiah, the ministry of John the Baptist; the blessed passion and precious death of Jesus Christ, His mighty resurrection and glorious ascension, Peter and Paul and the early Church, all contributed heavily to the further fulfillment of God's Plan. Popes, bishops, martyrs, saints, schisms, denominations, and others who have served, sacrificed, guided and directed different eras of Church History have all helped to reveal in great and small ways God's Plan for the salvation of our souls. Now this is our turn. The baton has been passed to us in our time and in our era, and it is now our responsibility; and it is an awesome responsibility as we assume our role in the salvation of the world.

While we go about our day often oblivious to this responsibility, the Lord God longs for us to bear witness to this history and to work with Him to move all of creation closer to the Kingdom. One key is to understand that Salvation History is a living history. It has not reached a dead end nor has it reached a plateau, but continues to be written through individuals and people of the present day. The bible is the living, breathing Word of God and it is forever relevant. Another key is to understand that the Lord God has distributed spiritual gifts to each of His people for the building up of the Kingdom on earth; as Paul puts it, *"...for the common good."* This responsibility falls on each one of us, and the spirituality of the present time remains dependent upon our willingness to use our God-given, Spirit-filled gifts to advance the Kingdom (1).

Modern day people such as Billy Graham, Martin Luther King, Jr. and Pope John XXIII answered the call and they are examples of present day prophets whose influences still affect present spirituality. But minor prophets also proclaim God's word mostly on the local scene; a dynamic pastor, a Sunday School Teacher, or a committed Vestry Member can all serve as prophets in their own parish. These are all examples of people using their God-given gifts for the building up of the Kingdom. It is the same Spirit which is available to you. They had one hundred percent of the Holy Spirit available to them and you have one hundred percent of the Holy Spirit available to you. The only difference is the depth and intensity of their response. In your own way and with the help of the Holy Spirit, you are capable of greatly influencing the people of the present day.

Spiritual gifts are too numerous to mention here especially without proper definition, but they can be found in part in the writings of Paul in Romans 11 and 12, and in 1 Corinthians 12 and 14. They are also well defined in a Spiritual Gifts Inventory available at any Christian Book Store (2). Through our Baptism, it becomes our responsibility to discover the gifts we possess and to seek ways to use them for His glory and for His purpose. I highly encourage you to take a Spiritual Gifts Inventory. This will help you to identify your gifts, it will offer a proper definition, and it will perhaps even suggest ways to use them.

It is incorrect to think that Church work is reserved for a select few. Paul makes it very clear that each person has been endowed with spiritual gifts and God expects each person to work with Him and share in the one ministry of His Son, Jesus Christ. There is an old Church adage that 20% of the people do 80% of the work. This should not be true. Through our Baptism, we assume the responsibility of identifying our spiritual gifts and putting them to proper use. Each baptized person is a member of the Church, and every member is a minister. This is another reason why Baptism is present tense.

"The gifts he gave were that some would be apostles, some prophets, some evangelists, some pastors and teachers, to equip the saints for the work of ministry, for building up the Body of Christ, until all of us come to the unity of the faith and the knowledge of the Son of God, to maturity, to the measure of the full stature of Christ," (Ephesians 4: 11-14).

It is evident that the work of building up the Kingdom will continue until we finally reach the Kingdom where everything will be realized and reach their fulfillment. We will reach the *full stature of Christ* only when we are one with Him. Until then there is plenty of work for everyone and there can be no slacking off. We must make sure that future generations are given the same hope as has been given to us. There is another old Church adage that the Church is never more than a generation away from being extinct. Each of us must ask ourselves, "What am I doing to make sure this does not happen?" According to our **Book of Common Prayer,** "The mission of the Church is to restore all people to unity with God and each other in Christ," (855). This unity will only be achieved in the oneness with the Son of God. Until then we remain a work in progress, but it must remain a goal to which we remain faithful.

Our son is a gear head who loves boats. If you get him on the topic of boat motors, his quiet and shy personality turns into a walking encyclopedia of marine mechanics, makes and models, horsepower and torque, props and performance, from single engine two strokes to cabin cruisers. He has become a sponge of the nuts and bolts that powers things through the water.

A couple in my parish owns a yacht building company and invited the two of us to visit their facility. Our son was so excited that he could not sleep the night before. When we arrived, we were both impressed with the size of the complex. Cindy met us and began to show us around. There were ten large bays where boats of all shapes and sizes were in different stages of having work done on them. Cindy explained each one as we walked along. One was having an engine overhauled. One was having the galley updated. Another was having the hull repainted. This went on all the way down the line. Finally, Anthony asked, "Do you build any new stuff?" Cindy replied, "Yes, in the last bay there is a new yacht being built." She could tell by the look on Anthony's face that he was a little surprised that only one new boat was being built which led Cindy to add, "Ninety percent of the work we do is restoration." I chimed in, "Hey, that's like the work I do in Church! Ninety percent of it is restoration!"

Again, "The mission of the Church is to *restore* all people to unity with God and each other in Christ." The Church, too, is in the restoration business. Our mission is to restore the relationship with our Father which has had a wedge driven through it by our sin. By using your spiritual gifts, you contribute to the mission of the Church rooted in Christ and at one with the Father not only for yourself, but for all of us. What greater purpose can life hold? Your primary goal in life should be to embrace our history, proclaim it to the present generation, and pave the road for future ones; if not you then whom? God needs you. He has confidence in you. He would not have equipped you with such gifts if He did not think you could be of good use to Him. You need to have that confidence in yourself.

And now, brothers, I beg you through the mercy of God to offer your bodies as a living sacrifice holy and acceptable to God, which is your spiritual worship. Do not conform yourselves to this age but be transformed by the renewal of your mind, so that you may judge what is God's will, what is good, pleasing and perfect," (Romans 12: 1,2).

We worship God by offering our bodies as a sacrifice to Him. For years I struggled with this passage because it seems to imply false martyrdom; that I should find a way to die for the faith. But this is not Paul's intention. Sacrifice here means servanthood. We worship God by becoming His servant and by being the servant of Jesus Christ. We honor God by surrendering our bodies to God to be used for His purpose. We best do this by conforming our minds to the spiritual world and not to this world, by entering into God's world and getting out of our own, and by sharing in the one, restorative mission of our Lord and Savior; by using our spiritual gifts to enhance the Kingdom.

There was an urgency in the early Church. Those early disciples, including Paul thought that the Second Coming was going to take place within their lifetime. Paul writes, *"See, now is the acceptable time, see, now is the day of salvation,"* (2 Corinthians 6:2). He literally meant that salvation was close at hand; that the Lord would return any day. This was Paul's motivating force; to baptize as many people as he could before this transpired. This was the passion of his missionary journeys, and this is why he and his other brothers and sisters in Christ were willing to suffer so much for the sake of the Kingdom. Their evangelism and indeed, their lives, were centered around the urgency of John the Baptist's message, "Prepare the way of the Lord." It is interesting that John the Baptist as well as Paul and the early disciples all understood that the way to prepare for the Lord is to repent and to be baptized.

The present day Church has lost much of that urgency. In fact, we must be careful not to become complacent. After 2000 years and still no Second Coming, we often think that the day of salvation is so far down the road that it should not consume us; it is another generation's concern. Even those in the present day who try to put a date on the end of time are met with skepticism and ridicule.

But Paul's words take on new meaning for us. The day of salvation is the day each of us accepts Jesus Christ as our Lord and Savior. Hopefully this is the day we are baptized, but for many, including those who were baptized as infants, this day comes much later. This is part of what John the Baptist meant when he proclaimed, *I baptize you with water; but one who is more powerful than I is coming; I am not worthy to untie the thong of his sandals. He will baptize you with the Holy Spirit and fire," (Luke 3:16).*

This does not imply that we need two Baptisms, but rather, the awakening of the Holy Spirit generally comes much later then the Baptism with water. Few have real life encounters such as when St. Paul was baptized in Acts 9 when water and the Spirit come simultaneously. While Baptism is the next logical step of accepting Christ in your heart, sometimes this sequence is reversed. There are many baptized people who do not have a personal relationship with the Lord. This needs to be the urgency of the present generation and in a way, we are doing catch up work; leading those who are already baptized to intimacy with the Lord. It is only then that their lives will change. It is then that our spiritual gifts will fulfill their purpose. This must be our urgency if the Church is going to be there for future generations, including our children.

I believe it frustrates God after He has devised a plan for the salvation of the world, put the right people in the right place at the right time with the right spiritual gifts, only to have these people ignore their gifts or use them for worldly profit. He must throw His Almighty hands in the air in disbelief. It's as though we do not want to save ourselves. Why be baptized?

We need to remind ourselves that The Gifts of the Holy Spirit are just that...Gifts. And they are given to be used and not put on a shelf or used solely for personal gain. How much of our lives is spent not understanding this connection. Instead of using our God-given gifts to build up the Kingdom, we use our gifts to get ahead in this world and often times, the spiritual world is left behind. Satan has made the lure of money irresistible and insatiable and we end up using our God-given gifts in the opposite way in which God intended them to be used.

But when we make the connection, and we begin to live a life in the Spirit, what incredible things begin to happen. It is like putting on a pair of spiritual 3-D glasses. A person begins to see the world in a whole new way and God's blessings are showered upon that person; some of these blessings result in material success, but most of them are spiritual enlightenments, epiphanies whereby God reveals more and more of Himself. This is what Paul speaks of in the above passage from Romans 12. It is a transformation from the way we used to live and the way we used to see things, to the way God wants us to live and the way in which God sees things. This is the original design of creation. It is a transformation from using our bodies for our own desires to using our bodies for God's desires.

You have been created out of God's love for a purpose. You have been given a unique combination of spiritual gifts that no one else has. So how are you using them? The Lord God needs you to use these gifts for His purpose. The Lord God is depending upon you to respond to His call.

"The harvest is plentiful, but the laborers are few; therefore ask the Lord of the harvest to send out laborers into his harvest," (Matthew 9: 37,38).

"Then I heard the voice of the Lord saying, 'Whom shall I send, and who will go for us?' And I said, 'Here I am, Lord. Send me,'" (Isaiah 6:8).

This is our turn in the History of Salvation.
This is your turn.
Baptism is present tense.

Questions

1. This is our turn in Salvation History. How are you contributing to the faith during our time?
2. Do you truly believe that you have 100% of God's Holy Spirit available to you? Do you truly believe that you have just as much of the Holy Spirit available to you as did the great prophet Isaiah, or the disciple Paul, or Billy Graham, or MLK, Jr.? Do you really believe that? If not, why not? Would God withhold any of Himself from you? If so, what are you doing with it?
3. Which spiritual gifts do you know you possess and which ones do you think you might possess?
4. Have you ever taken a Spiritual Gifts Inventory? If so, what did the inventory reveal that was surprising to you? If not, why don't you commit to taking one?
5. The Church is in the restoration business. How can God use you to restore the part of the world in which you live?
6. There was such an urgency in the early Church because they thought that The Second Coming was going to happen very soon. The present day Church has lost that urgency. What effect do you think this has had on present day faith?
7. Do you truly believe that God needs you to carry on His work in the world?

Section VII

Death and Resurrection

*"Do you not know that all of us who have been bap-
tized into Christ Jesus were baptized into His death?
Therefore we have been buried with Him by baptism
into death, so that, just as Christ was raised from the
dead by the glory of the Father, so we too might walk
in newness of life," (Romans 6: 3,4).*

aptism into the death of Christ Jesus is essential to
our understanding of the sacrament. It is absolutely
essential. And for Christians, it has a few different meanings:
a) physical suffering and death, b) the death of surrender, and
c) the death of the flesh in order to live in the Spirit.

Physical Suffering and Death

As mentioned earlier, one of the biggest myths about following the Lord Christ is that life will be free of problems and
suffering. Some people tend to think that this is part of God's

side of the bargain. This myth explains why some faithful followers become upset with the Lord when tragic events happen to them. "Why me? How can this happen? How does this fit into Your plan for me?" In The Parable of the Sower, it is the seed which falls on rocky ground that springs up at first but when hardship is encountered and because there are no roots, it withers and dies, (Matt. 13:20, 21). Such Christians tend to develop the attitude that the Lord is not living up to His end of the covenant. This can even lead to some resentment, even anger toward the Lord. It has been my experience while working with people undergoing great suffering that while some will not question the Lord at all, others will abandon the faith altogether. This is why understanding the above passage from Romans 6 is so essential.

We would do well to remember that pain, suffering, and death were not part of God's original design of creation, but rather, they entered humanity after the fall of Adam and Eve (1 Corinth. 15:21). These evils in the world are a direct result of the sin of our first parents and to which we continue to contribute.

"God did not make death, and he does not delight in the death of the living. For he created all things so that they might exist; the generative forces of the world are wholesome, and there is no destructive poison in them, and the dominion of Hades is not on earth. For righteousness is immortal. For God created us for incorruption, and made us in the image of his own eternity, but through the devil's envy death entered the world, and those who belong to his company experience it," (Wisdom 1:13-15; 2:23,24: Proper 8 B).

As Paul reminds us in The Book of Romans, *"The wages of sin is death,"* (6:23). The suffering and death in the world, therefore, are none of the Lord's doing. The suffering in the world is a result of the evils in the world. God gets blamed for a lot of things that God doesn't do. To imagine a world free of suffering and death is to imagine a world free of sin; which is to imagine the Kingdom.

With this understanding, Paul had a very different attitude toward suffering (1). This is because he understood that the suffering Jesus endured did not come from His Father. Jesus was not immune from suffering just because He was the Son of God. Jesus experienced suffering just as we do. Jesus was like us in every way but sin. In our **Book of Common Prayer,** *The Proper Preface for Lent* prays, *"Jesus Christ our Lord; who was tempted in every way as we are, yet did not sin. By his grace we are able to triumph over every evil, and to live no longer for ourselves alone, but for him who died for us and rose again,"* (379).

Jesus shows us that it is indeed possible to live as a human and not sin. He was tempted just as strongly as we are, but He did not give into the desires of the evil one. Jesus was 100% human and His divinity did not detract from His humanity which means that He was the perfect human. He was humanity in its purest form. Jesus is what the Father had in mind when the Father created each of us. There is no excuse for sinning. It is only because we have come to accept it about ourselves and we have caved in to Satan's temptations so often that we have easily fallen into his prey. We have a fallen nature, but not a sinful nature. Sin is in direct opposition to the nature in which we were created.

Even though Jesus never sinned, He still encountered the effects of sin, which include suffering and death. If Jesus were immune from human suffering then we would not be able to relate to Him as our Lord and Savior, and we would have a right to complain about our suffering. Instead, Jesus was mired in the pain with which all humans suffer and remained obedient until death, even death on a cross (Phil. 2:8).

Paul linked his personal suffering to the suffering of Christ. If the Innocent One of God was not excused from the suffering He endured, then why should we, who are guilty, complain about ours? Paul begins this passage from Romans 6 by asking, *Do you not know this....?* Essentially he is asking, *"Isn't this evident? Isn't it elementary?"*

In addition, Paul understood that Jesus is stronger than the suffering. *"I consider the suffering of the present to be as nothing compared to the glory to be revealed in us,"* (Rom. 8:18). Eventually the suffering will be conquered. Eventually we will be led to the fullness of God's healing grace. What can help us through times of suffering is the confidence that Jesus will eventually win. He will eventually lead us to a place of comfort and peace. This too shall pass. *"Commit your way to the Lord, trust in Him and He will act,"* (Psalm 37:5). So for Paul, it is not a matter of being excused from the suffering. It is rather a matter of asking the Lord for the endurance to see it through knowing that victory will eventually triumph.

I love those days that begin with overcast skies and even some rain in the morning, but then turn sunny in the afternoon. Those days remind us of storms in our lives which we encounter; times of trial and tribulation and suffering. But if you press into the Lord and stay by His side, He will lead you to sunny skies and brighter days. There is always hope. The Lord will always remain faithful even when you cannot recognize His presence in the midst of the storm.

If we are not immune from the suffering then we are also not immune from death. Death is a necessary evil if we are to inherit the Kingdom, which is the goal of Baptism. Through Jesus, death has meaning and purpose; it is the path through which we have hope for the Kingdom. The sole purpose of the cocoon is for the caterpillar to be transformed into a butterfly. Likewise, Baptism into His death is the adoption process by which we become children of God and heirs to the Kingdom (Rom. 8:14ff). Without Jesus, there is no hope. Without Jesus, death has no meaning. And without Baptism, there is no life in Jesus.

Baptism then is intimately linked to death and new life. A baptized person accepts this connection. But unless you accept this connection and are baptized, death remains, but it does not result in new life. Paul refers to Baptism as a "Baptism into Jesus' death" in order to share in His glory. Through Baptism, death is a passageway to new life. You die once, but you do not stay dead. You are led to new life. The caterpillar does not remain in the cocoon, but it is transformed into new life. In **The Book of Common Prayer,** The Proper Preface for a Burial prays in part, *"For Your faithful people, O Lord, life is changed, not ended; and when our mortal body lies in death, there is prepared for us a dwelling place eternal in the heavens,"* (**BCP,** 382).

This is the power of Baptism by full submersion. In it, the baptized person is fully submersed under the water. This is a symbol of dying; "Baptism into the death of Christ." When the baptized person comes up out of the water, it is symbol of resurrection, the new life in Christ. We die in Christ so as to be raised with Him. I wish more Episcopal Churches used full submersion. It is a vivid symbol. However, many/ most Episcopal Churches elect to pour water over the head of the baptized person. It is poured over the head three times; in the name of the Father, and of the Son, and of the Holy Spirit. While the thrice pouring holds an important Trinitarian meaning, the symbol of death and resurrection is lost and the new life in Christ is relegated to the Baptismal Instruction; like this one.

The Death of Surrender

There is a second kind of death which a Christian must undergo; this is the death of surrender. The death of surrender contributes greatly in making Baptism present tense because unlike physical death which happens once, the death of surrender is a daily struggle to live a life according to God's Will and not our will. The power of surrender is the power of freedom. Let go and let God; trust. Baptism is the key of a relationship based on trust which is often difficult for humans to maintain. Surrendering your life to Christ is a daily decision while facing the temptations of the evil one who wants control as well. Baptism is the first step toward total surrender.

Surrender is not easy but the effects are obvious. This was once the topic of an adult bible study I was leading and a man who was a retired Army Lieutenant Colonel, a man of great faith, a veteran of Viet Nam, a man I truly admired began revealing how his older daughter had been a problem child her entire life. His heart was absolutely broken because she was presently an addict and walking far from the Lord. He explained that he and his wife had done everything they could possibly do for her and she was not responding to their love or to their help. I suggested that they should surrender their daughter to the Lord Christ. After all, what they were doing was not working. He replied, "I'm retired Army so surrender is not easy." He continued, "I have been in very difficult combat situations and never surrendered. It is ironic that my daughter could lead me to wave the white flag. I have surrendered her to Jesus...a hundred times." "A hundred times?" I asked. "That means you have taken her back a hundred and one times because if you had truly surrendered her to Christ, you would not still be trying to fix her. Let me tell you, Scott," I continued. "You are facing an enemy much stronger than you have ever encountered before. This is not physical combat. This is spiritual combat and you do not have the ability to fight off this enemy. Only Jesus does and unless you totally surrender her to Him right now, you will lose this battle and your daughter with it."

At that moment the Holy Spirit rushed into that room and for the next hour we experienced an amazing spiritual presence. I was reminded a little bit of what the apostles must have experienced on that first Pentecost Sunday. It was amazing, and transforming, and absolutely powerfully spiritual. There is something about surrender that is very spiritual. It certainly was the key to that experience.

Jesus says, *"Whoever loves father or mother more than me is not worthy of me; and who ever loves son or daughter more than me is not worthy of me; and whoever does not take up the cross and follow me is not worthy of me. Those who find their life will lose it, and those who lose their life for my sake will find it,"* (Matt. 10: 37-39).

Baptism must change the way we think. We must begin to think like Jesus. *"Let the same mind be in you that was in Christ Jesus."* Remember that line? Paul says, the same mind as Jesus. Think of the way in which Jesus could have thought of Himself. He could have thought; "I am the Son of God. I do not have to take any of their garbage." He could have thought, "I am saving these people from eternal death. They owe me big time." He could have thought, "If these people only knew who it is they are dealing with." But this is not the way Jesus thought or operated in the world. We are willing to praise Him and glorify Him, but rarely truly imitate Him. Too much of our self gets in the way. We want things our way. Many people are humble, but not a servant. Jesus turns the world upside down. Baptism challenges us to change the way we think. Baptism challenges us to surrender.

The popular question, "What would Jesus do?"(WWJD) is a good question because it challenges us to consider how Jesus would react in a particular situation. I find myself in a particular situation and I should think about what Jesus would do if He were in the same situation. But the next step in our spiritual walk is the question, "How would Jesus think?" (HWJT). This is a transforming question because it eliminates the translation of how Jesus would act in a particular situation to a deeper, more fundamental process of entering into the way in which Jesus viewed the world. This is closer to the mind of Christ.

I was once in a conversation with a woman of Mexican descent who was a new comer to our parish. She had only been in America a short time and she spoke in broken English, carefully choosing her words making sure she was expressing herself properly. I asked her, "Do you think in Spanish and then translate into English?" She responded, "I did for a long time, but I am just now starting to think in English. It is very difficult and it has been a long process. I have spent my whole life thinking in Spanish and looking at everything from the Mexican culture. But I have learned to think like an American and the English has become easier."

The same is true with us. The question, "What would Jesus do?" requires a translation from a physical set of circumstances to the spiritual mindset of Christ. However, the question, "How would Jesus think?" puts us directly in touch with the mind of Christ and the spiritual world. This change of thought is very difficult and it is a long process, but it is transforming; the renewing of our minds. To think like Jesus thinks requires that we stop thinking like we think; from the culture and perspective in which we have been raised, and to change our perspective into that of Jesus, a humble and obedient servant.

The total surrender of your life to Christ is a daily struggle. Baptism is present tense. The times when we fall are those times when we try to do things on our own; by ourselves. It is difficult to do, but things work out much better when Christ is at the helm of your ship. It is just easier to let Him run things. It is easier to put Him in the front seat of your bicycle built for two and let Him steer. It demands trust, however, something which we mentioned in the previous chapter under The Gift of Faith.

The Lord Christ, the Son of God completely surrendered Himself over to His Father's Will and became a servant because His Father asked Him to do so. Could Jesus have rejected the mission His Father gave to Him? Yes, I suppose so because being God, the Son was perfectly free. But it would not have been in the nature of the Son to turn His back on His Father's Will. The Son understood that the salvation of the world could only come through Him. And if the Son of God became obedient to the Father for our salvation then we must become obedient to the Father as the recipients of the Son's atoning work. We must also reach a point where it would be against our nature to turn our backs on the Father. We must become His servant. We must surrender.

That is the power of surrender. It is not losing your freedom, it is gaining it by freely accepting the Father's Will. My Army friend viewed surrender as something negative, something to avoid at all costs. And in the physical world this is often true. This kind of surrender means you have encountered a force more powerful than yourself and you are giving up against your will. But to surrender your life to Christ is a positive decision that contains the freedom of admitting that you are incapable of living your life to the vision God had for you when He created you. Ask any recovering alcoholic in The Twelve Step Program and the first thing he/she will admit is that trying to run their own life is impossible. They need a Higher Authority to run their life for them. They need to surrender.

Death to the Flesh and Life in the Spirit

"For those who live according to the flesh set their minds on the things of the flesh, but those who live according to the Spirit set their minds on the things of the Spirit. To set the mind on the flesh is death, but to set the mind on the Spirit is life and peace. For this reason the mind that is set on the flesh is hostile to God; it does not submit to God's law-indeed it cannot, and those who are in the flesh cannot please God, (Rom. 8:5-8).

"Live by the Spirit, I say, and do not gratify the desires of the flesh. For what the flesh desires is opposed to the Spirit, and what the Spirit desires is opposed to the flesh; for these are opposed to each other, to prevent you from doing what you want. But if you are led by the Spirit, you are not subject to the law. Now the works of the flesh are obvious: fornication, impurity, licentiousness, idolatry, sorcery, enmities, strife,

jealousy, anger, quarrels, dissentions, factions, envy, drunk-
enness, carousing, and things like these. I am warning you
like I warned you before, those who do such things
will not inherit the Kingdom of God.

By contrast, the fruit of the Spirit is love, joy peace, patience,
kindness, generosity, faithfulness, gentleness and self-con-
trol. There is no law against such things. And those who
belong to Christ Jesus have crucified the flesh with its
passions and desires. If we live by the Spirit let us also be
guided by the Spirit," (Galatians 5: 16-25).

A third form of surrender a Christian must undergo at
Baptism is one of the major mind transformations to which
Paul calls us. And that is to stop thinking of our bodies as
simply flesh, but "to present our bodies to God as our spiritual worship." This has powerful meaning and it has taken on
a profoundness to me in recent years. The body is not simply
flesh, it is a work of eternal art.

"For you yourself created my inmost parts;
You knit me together in my mother's womb.
I will thank you because I am marvelously made;
Your works are wonderful, and I know it well,"
(Psalm 139: 12,13).

The body God has created for each of us is beautiful. It
does not matter what others think of you in this regard, God
thinks that you are beautiful. And yet the flesh of the body is
the cause of most sin. How disappointing this must be to God,
our Creator. He created our bodies as beautiful and life giving,
artfully designing each one with His creative powers so that

from the beginning of human time, no two have ever been the same. And yet we abuse them and sin with them through lusts, perversions, gluttony, obesity, alcohol and drug abuse, physical and verbal abuse, prostitution, piercing and tattoos with a satanic purpose, cutting, suicide, and a variety of other ways. We lust after another's body and we forget that the one over whom we lust is a child of God, and Jesus thinks of that person is a completely different way. How sad this is. We need a transformation of the mind.

It is a real shame that the body is left behind when we die. This beautiful piece of eternal art becomes, well …disposable. That is not the way it was originally designed. What a shame. What a waste. And what is worse is that many true Christians, those who have a firm belief in the resurrection have also begun to think of their bodies as disposable, as not worth very much and thus, the original intent of the body by God has lost tremendous purpose.

Paul appeals to us to use our bodies as our spiritual worship. We worship God through the way we use our bodies; through what we do and say and think – yes, the brain is part of the body. We are to use our bodies to worship the Lord God through song and good deeds, proclaiming the name of the Lord Christ every place we go. We are the hands and feet of Jesus in the world. We are the proclaimers of the Good News by word and example. We are the mindset of Christ who views the world through the lenses of His Father. Everything we do and say and think is marked by our Baptism. Baptism is present tense.

It is a shame that we leave our bodies behind when we die, but at this point, it is a necessity in order to enter the Kingdom. All of the great saints understood this and while some of them may have taken care of themselves physically, their focus was always on the spirit. "Live for today," is a scheme of the evil one who seeks to devour us. We are called to enjoy this life but never to abuse it. And although the Gospels fall short in telling us how much Jesus enjoyed His humanity, He had to have certainly done so. Life is good. There is much joy in living. Allow the spirit to guide the body and don't get things backward.

When we reach this point in our spiritual walk, our flesh and our spirit begin to work in harmony with each other instead of fighting each other. When our spirit becomes that of a humble, obedient servant and our flesh is aligned with our spirit, then we are closer to the original design with which God created each of us and our flesh will begin to reap the fruits of the spirit as outlined in Galatians 5: 22, 23. When we begin to think like Jesus then we will begin to live like Him.

Instead of looking in the mirror and focusing on your faults, look in the mirror and focus on the beauty with which God created you. Noticing your faults only looks at the physical while seeing your beauty also considers your heart and soul. This is the way God sees you. And when you have the mind of God it becomes easier to surrender everything to Him.

Death and new life, suffering and pain, obedience and sacrifice, humility and surrender are all essential themes for Baptism. There is no way to prepare anyone for all of it, for Baptism is something that we must always live into. But the moment of Baptism, the moment when one publically accepts Jesus Christ as his/her Lord and Savior is the first step in a life-long quest to know Him more profoundly to love Him more deeply in appreciation of His love for you, and to live a life in anticipation of the Kingdom. Baptism must transform our lives into a new, spiritual way of thinking and must serve as a reference point in everything we do. Baptism is present tense.

Questions

1. Was it a shock to you to learn that Baptism in Christ Jesus was a Baptism into His death?
2. Pain, suffering and death were not part of God's original design of creation. However, when these occur, do you find yourself still blaming God?
3. When you are in the midst of pain and suffering, do you truly believe that God will eventually heal you? Do you ever wonder, "What is taking Him so long?"
4. If you have surrendered your life to God and are living in the Spirit then you should be reaping the Fruits of the Spirit as described in Galatians 5. Give witness whether or not you have completely surrendered.
5. How have you surrendered your life to Christ?
6. What in the flesh is keeping you from a life in the Spirit?
7. It is a shame that the body is left behind when we die because it is an eternal work of art from the Creator. How are you caring for your body?

Section VIII

The Baptismal Covenant

"Days are coming, says the Lord, when I will make a new covenant with the house of Israel and with the house of Judah. It will not be like the covenant I made with their fathers the day that I took them by the hand to lead them forth from the land of Egypt; for they broke my covenant and I grew weary of them, says the Lord. But this is the covenant I will make with the house of Israel after those days, says the Lord; I will place my law in their minds and I will write them upon their hearts; I will be their God and they shall be my people," (Heb. 8:8-10).

Through The Baptismal Covenant, God renews His relationship with His people. The Covenant made through Abraham which the Israelites continually broke and over whom the Lord became weary is now renewed through The Covenant of Baptism. And there are some expectations on God's part. He expects His people to remain faithful to this new covenant. As He recreates the world through His Son,

Jesus Christ, He recreates His people by means of a new covenant. It is ours not to break, but to remain faithful. The Lord God has written His law on our minds for us to know what He demands, and He has written it on our hearts for us to love what He demands.

> *"Almighty God, you alone can bring into order the unruly wills and affections of sinners: Grant your people grace to love what you command and desire what you promise; that, among the swift and varied changes of the world, our hearts may surely there be fixed where true joys are to be found; through Jesus Christ our Lord, who lives and reigns with you and the Holy Spirit, one God, now and forever. Amen."*
>
> (Proper Preface for The Fifth Sunday in Lent, **BCP,** 219)

But are we any better than the unruly Israelites? Are we once again making God weary because His people refuse to remain faithful? Are we in any better shape than the Israelites of old? In one sense, we could be worse off because we know more. We have so much more of God's revelation available to us. The more you know, the more you are held responsible. One of the reasons that Baptism is present tense is because we must continually strive to remain faithful to the new covenant in the midst of the world's temptations. And God expects us to remain faithful. Faithfulness is non-negotiable.

The renewal of The Baptismal Covenant begins in The **BCP** at the bottom of page 303 and I have divided it into three parts: 1) The Witness of the Congregation, 2) The Baptismal Covenant, and, 3) The Five Difficult Questions.

The Witness of the Congregation

Q. Will you who witness these vows do all in your power to support *these persons* in *their* life in Christ?

A. We will. (**BCP,** 303)

There are three important comments regarding the congregation's witness to the one being baptized. 1) The congregation is committing itself to the spiritual well being of the individual. This means that if a member of the congregation ever notices that the person being baptized begins to stray, that congregant will intervene. This is very similar to the congregation's commitment at The Sacrament of Marriage (**BCP,** 425). While these are nice words to say and are necessary for the ceremony to continue, do we actually take this commitment seriously, either at a Marriage or at a Baptism? Are we truly willing to step in when we notice that something is not right? 2) Because of the congregation's commitment, it would be best if the individual is baptized in his/her home church. Take the example of someone who is from out of town, perhaps a relative of someone in your parish who wants to be baptized in your church. So then, how does your congregation make a commitment to someone they will rarely see? This may not the best case scenario unless you view the congregation as a representative of the larger Church. Perhaps a better scenario would be for the person to be baptized in his/her home parish. 3) It is amazing how God can work. He can use the Baptism of a single individual to have the entire congregation renew its Baptismal Covenant. This is especially true if the one being baptized is an infant. God can use that little baby to touch the hearts of everyone present.

The Baptismal Covenant

(**BCP,** 304)

Using *The Apostles Creed,* the congregation reaffirms its statement of faith. The congregation renews its covenant with God. The Apostles Creed is a personal statement of faith and it is used at Baptism and Morning Prayer (**BCP:** Rite I, 53 and Rite II, 96). The Apostles Creed was not written by the apostles but is based on what the apostles taught. The Nicene Creed is a communal statement of faith and is used at The Holy Eucharist (**BCP:** Rite I, 326 and Rite II, 358). Both creeds are Trinitarian in nature confirming our belief in God the Father, God the Son, and God the Holy Spirit. They serve as the foundation of **The Catechism (BCP,** 843-862). The Apostles and Nicene Creeds, and The Catechism serve as the doctrine of our faith.

The Apostles Creed contains the following 12 tenants of our doctrine:

1. I believe in God the Father, Almighty, Maker of heaven and earth:
2. And in Jesus Christ, His Only Begotten Son, our Lord:
3. Who was conceived by the Holy Ghost, born of the Virgin Mary:
4. Suffered under Pontius Pilate; was crucified, died and was buried; He descended into hell:
5. On the third day He rose again:
6. He ascended into heaven, and sits at the right hand of the Father:
7. He will come again to judge the living and the dead:

8. I believe in the Holy Spirit:
9. The holy catholic church:
10. The forgiveness of sin:
11. The resurrection of the body
12. And life everlasting. Amen. (1)

Five Difficult Questions

(**BCP,** 304-305)

Though not listed as such, I believe the five questions which follow The Apostles Creed are the most difficult in the Prayer Book. This is the crux of God's desire to renew His covenant with His people. Each time a person is baptized, the entire congregation renews the covenant between God and His people which is the desire of God in the Hebrews passage (2).

Q1. Will you continue in the apostles' teaching and fellowship, in the breaking of the bread, and in the prayers?

A. I will, with God's help.

The "apostles' teaching" is the doctrine of faith proclaimed by the creeds which forms the fellowship or community of believers. God expects us to remain faithful to these tenants of faith and to remain faithful to the community of believers. Again, faithfulness is not negotiable. We are also obliged to further our knowledge of the Lord through reading and studying the scriptures on a regular basis, both on our own and with other members of the community. The more we know the Lord, the more we are able to love Him. Baptism is only the beginning of our spiritual formation. Sunday Eucharist needs to be enhanced by the enlightenment of the scriptures through weekly study.

"Blessed Lord, who has caused all holy Scriptures to be written for our learning: Grant us so to hear them, read, mark, and learn, and inwardly digest them, that we may embrace and ever hold fast the blessed hope of ever lasting life, which you have given us in our Savior Jesus Christ ; who lives and reigns with you and the Holy Spirit, one God, forever and ever. Amen,"

(Collect for Proper 28; **BCP,** 236).

"Breaking of the bread" of course, refers to the Eucharist. The disciples on the road to Emmaus recognized Jesus in the breaking of the bread (Luke 24: 13-35). True intimacy with Jesus comes in the consumption of His Body and Blood in the Real Presence of Holy Communion. The congregation promises to continue attending Church and to receive Holy Communion. But then again, that is why they are there. Are we preaching to the choir?

"The prayers" are not only those which we pray during the course of the Eucharist, but also those that we pray at home with our families, and those we pray on our own. *"Rejoice always, pray without ceasing, give thanks in all circumstances; for this is the will of God in Christ Jesus for you,"* (1 Thess. 5: 16-19). Pray without ceasing...imagine. Prayer should consume our day; our day should not consume our prayers. The congregation promises...promises...to continue praying.

Q2. Will you persevere in resisting evil, and, whenever you
fall into sin, repent and return to the Lord?

A. I will, with God's help.

The Reconciliation of a Penitent (**BCP,** 447) is the means
of grace by which we make our way back to the Lord after
we have been unfaithful to the Baptismal Covenant. Thus, the
Baptismal Covenant and The Reconciliation of a Penitent are
intimately connected. It is the amazing love of God that we
are the ones who break the covenant by our sins and yet God
is the One Who provides the means by which we make our
way back to Him. How badly He wants us in a relationship
with Him.

Considering the Sacrament of Reconciliation, the
Episcopal Church teaches that all may; some should; and none
must. More clearly, all Christians may receive this sacrament,
some who are in serious sin should receive this sacrament, but
none must receive this sacrament. It cannot be made manda-
tory. Nevertheless, it has been my personal experience that
while the sacramental grace of repentance is very powerful
and uplifting, this Sacrament of Reconciliation is not widely
embraced. This is unfortunate. The priest is the representative of God and the community and this sacrament renews the
relationship with both. Sin offends God and disturbs the community. Both relationships need healing. A great example of
this is the story of Achan in Joshua 7.

The Sacrament of Reconciliation is yet another way in
which God renews His covenant with His people.

*"Almighty and everlasting God, who in the Paschal Mystery
established the new covenant of reconciliation: Grant that*

all who have been reborn into the fellowship of Christ's Body may show forth in their lives what they profess by their faith; through Jesus Christ our Lord, who lives and reigns with you and the Holy Spirit, one God, forever and ever. Amen."

(Collect for the Second Sunday of Easter, **BCP,** 224).

Each year on the Second Sunday of Easter, The Lectionary gives us the Gospel of the Doubting Thomas: (John 20: 19-31). And while preachers often focus on Thomas and his lack of faith, not to be overlooked is Jesus' institution of The Reconciliation of the Penitent. As part of the same Gospel, we hear, *"Receive the Holy Spirit. If you forgive the sins of any, they are forgiven. If you retain the sins of any, they are retained,"* (22,23). Confessing your sins and asking forgiveness for the ways in which you have been unfaithful to the Baptismal Covenant are directly linked to the Holy Spirit and provide the grace and mercy of the covenant's renewal.

A major part of repentance is the amendment of life. True repentance understands the offensiveness of sin and includes a concerted effort to avoid such sin in the future, to persevere in resisting evil. Without true amendment of life, God's grace is manipulated with the attitude that I can do whatever I want and God will always take me back. Sometimes even before we sin, we tell ourselves that afterwards we can simply ask for His forgiveness and He will be there for us. *"What are we to say? Should we continue in sin in order that grace may abound? By no means! How can we who died to sin go on living in it?"* (Rom. 6: 1,2). Repentance includes amendment. Perseverance in resisting evil is a daily struggle. Baptism is present tense.

Q3. Will you proclaim by word and example the Good News of God in Christ?

A. I will, with God's help.

"You are the salt of the earth; but if salt has lost its taste, how can its saltiness be restored? It is no longer good for anything, but is thrown out and trampled underfoot.

You are the light of the world. A city built on a hill cannot be hidden. No one after lighting a lamp puts it under the bushel basket, but on a lampstand, and it gives light to all in the house. In the same way, let your light shine before others, so they may see your good works, and give glory to your Father in heaven," (Matt. 5: 13-16).

Do you live your life proclaiming the Good News by word and example? Are you the salt of your earth? Are you the light of your world? I can't tell you how many times I have had the opportunity to give witness to Jesus Christ and I have allowed the moment to pass me by. Oh yeah, when I am wearing my collar it's easy. People expect it of me and I play the part well. But take the collar off and most often my mouth falls silent. The person who initiated the phrase to never talk about politics and religion was Satan. If Christians do not proclaim Christ, then who will?

One of my success stories, however, came at a gas station. I was pumping my gas in a pair of shorts and a tee shirt when I caught the eye of the guy who was at the pump directly across from me. I simply said, "Hi, how ya doin'?" I wasn't expecting much of a reply and hoping I wouldn't get one. You know, it's just the polite thing to do. When you catch someone's eyes like that you are like a deer caught in headlights. He responded, "Could be better." I said to myself, what have I gotten myself into? Now... I could have left it there and gone about my business, but I reluctantly pressed on and asked, "What's up?" This initiated a conversation during which he revealed that he had just been diagnosed with prostate cancer and that he was scheduled the next day for some additional tests. This guy was desperate for someone with whom to talk. I quickly realized that God had placed me there for a purpose. The Holy Spirit was at work. I was at that gas station at that pump at that time for a reason. A couple of minutes either way and we would have missed each other. This was no coincidence and the Spirit quickly revealed to me what was really going on..

We spoke for several minutes. I assured him that the cancer was detected because God wanted him to live. I asked him, given the choice, would he rather not know about the cancer and allow it to go undetected, or would he rather know about it in enough time to do something about it? He said that he would rather know about it so it could be treated. I then asked, "So what is the problem?" I assured him again that God wants him to live. I told him that if God had not revealed this to him then he would have felt better at the moment, but the long range effects would have been much worse.

Through the power of the Holy Spirit, I know that I was a comfort to him. I said a healing prayer with him right there at the gas pump. I really did not want him to know that I was a priest. I wanted to be just as mysterious to him as he was to me. I had never seen him before and I have never seen him since. Just a moment in time that was bonded through the love and healing power of Jesus Christ. I left feeling like salt. I left feeling like the light of Christ. As many times as I got it wrong, I got that one right. Opportunities like that present themselves everyday if we are open and tuned in. After that episode, I began stopping in a gas station with still a half to three-quarters of a tank asking, "How is everybody doing? Anybody sick?"

Q4. Will you seek and serve Christ in all persons, loving your neighbor as yourself?

A. I will, with God's help.

"Owe no one anything, except to love one another; for the one who loves another has fulfilled the law. The commandments, 'You shall not commit adultery; You shall not murder; You shall not steal; You shall not covet;' and any other commandment, are summed up in this word,

'Love your neighbor as yourself.' Love does no wrong to a neighbor; therefore, love is the fulfilling of the law,"
(Rom. 13: 8-12).

In Section VII: "Death and Resurrection," we were making the transition from, What Would Jesus Do? to, How Does Jesus Think? Paul told us that we should have the same mind as Christ Who was a *humble and obedient* servant. To love requires that we become humble and obedient, to see others as Christ sees them, to "seek and serve Christ in all persons." But this question goes a step further. It demands that we love our neighbor as much as we love ourselves.

In the Parable of the Good Samaritan (Luke 10: 25-37), the lawyer, wanting to justify himself, asks, "And who is my neighbor?" The lawyer's motive is to justify himself. He seeks to love according to his own standards and not by Jesus' standards. He is serving himself. He is not seeking and serving Christ. The lawyer seeks to put limitations and boundaries on those whom he loves and he wants Jesus to identify a small circle of people whom he should love. I said before, love is designed to be given away. The natural flow of love is outward, away from yourself. Any love that you keep for yourself become selfish and perverted. It's like keeping something in the refrigerator too long; it becomes moldy and mildewed and must be thrown away. This is what the lawyer wanted.

Of the five difficult questions, perhaps this is the most difficult one. To love your neighbor as much as you love yourself is to understand that everyone is just as important in the eyes of God as you are. Arrogance must be replaced with humility. Self righteousness must be replaced with honesty. Prejudice must be replaced with equality. Apathy must be met with compassion. And the capacity of Jesus to love must serve as the model of our own love. *"In the end three things remain; faith, hope, and love; and the greatest of these is love,"* (1 Corinth. 13: 13). St. Augustine wrote, "Love...and do whatever else you want," (3)

Q5. Will you strive for justice and peace among all people, and respect the dignity of every human being?

A. I will, with God's help.

Directly related to Question 4 is Question 5. While the first three questions are directed inward and our own spirituality, these last two questions are directed outward and our relationships with others. A similar format is found in the Ten Commandments; the first three commandments address our relationship with God and the remaining seven address our relationship with others. It is in our love for others that we reflect the love of Christ. We become a mirror. God looks at us and sees our love for others, and others look at us and see our love for God.

Justice, peace, respect, and dignity form the core of our love for others. I have a very good friend who owns four fast food restaurants and who is about to open a fifth. He is a simple Georgia boy with the heart of gold and a very good family man. "Quite the entrepreneur," I once said to him. He told me, "When you own a restaurant, there are some things that you need to know, but other than that, it's really quite easy. The first rule I tell my employees is that no matter who you are addressing, you do so with dignity and respect. You know, that comes back to you. What goes around comes around."

Philosopher Martin Buber wrote that we form two kinds of relationships: I-It and I-Thou (4). In an I-It relationship we treat the other as an object; as being inferior to us. This opens the door to manipulation, degradation, pornography and prostitution, gossip, bullying, and a myriad of other ways in which we use people for selfish purposes. In an I-Thou relationship we treat the other as an equal, as having the same God-given dignity and respect with which He created each of us. Humility is a by-product of I-Thou relationships. It would be a great exercise for you to consider your interpersonal relationships and determine which is which. Loving your neighbor as much as you love yourself demands I-Thou relationships.

John tells us,

> *"Those who say, 'I love God,' and hate their brothers or sisters, are liars; for those who do not love a brother or sister*

*whom they have seen, cannot love God whom they have not
seen. The commandment we have from him is this; those who
love God must love their brothers and sisters also,"*
(1 John 4: 20,21).

In the previous section, Section VII: Death and
Resurrection, we were talking about how sad it is that the
body is left behind at death. That is because each body is an
eternal work of art; each person is the result of God's creative
energy. Humans are finely sculptured pieces of glass that are
easily broken if not handled properly.

You would never stand in front of a painting by Picasso
and criticize it. Even if you did not like his style, you would
not say anything out of respect of the artist and his reputation. In like manner, we have no right to judge or criticize the
creative, eternal work of God. Each of us is a unique piece of
God's eternal art. Even if you don't like His style on a couple
of His pieces, it is better not to say anything out of respect for
the Artist. Love is the key. It is the one motive which put us in
direct contact with the heart of God.

***

As I said from the outset, these are difficult questions not
to be taken lightly. But God expects faithfulness and when we
fall, He provides a means to return. And as I said previously,
Baptism is something into which we are constantly living. We
are never quite there. And as I have on more than one occasion, Baptism is present tense.

Questions

1. The opening passage from Hebrews proclaims that the Israelites broke God's covenant so often that God became weary of them. Have you ever had a child or a friend who broke ties with you so often that you became weary of them? Do you better understand what it is like to be God? What other emotions do you think God experiences?

2. Are we any better than the early Israelites who made God weary?

3. In the Witness of the Congregation, the people vow their support to the person being baptized. Do you take this commitment seriously or are they just nice words that you say?

4. In the 12 tenets of our faith as proclaimed in The Apostles Creed, are there any with which you disagree or find difficult to accept?

5. Have you ever received The Reconciliation of a Penitent? If so, describe the feeling you had when you were done. If not, why not? What is keeping you from this incredible source of grace?

6. I explained an incredible situation that I had at a gas station. It was just a moment in time. Can you give witness to such a moment?

7. Do you strive for justice and peace among all people?

Section IX

The Baptism

"And Jesus came to them and said to them, 'All authority in heaven and on earth has been given to me. Go therefore, and make disciples of all nations, baptizing them in the name of the Father and of the Son and of the Holy Spirit, and teaching them to obey everything that I have commanded you. And remember, I am with you always, to the end of the age,'"

(Matt. 28: 19, 20).

The above passage is called, "The Great Commission." It is Jesus' final instructions to His disciples prior to His Ascension. The Good News of Jesus' death for our sins and resurrection to new life had to be proclaimed to the world and Jesus commissions His disciples for this ministry. We are reminded of the Post Communion Prayer, "And now, Father, send us out to do the work you have given us to do," (**BCP,** 365). The work is to further spread the Gospel by making more disciples, and the way to make disciples is through Baptism. This is our turn.

The Prayers for the Candidate (**BCP,** 305), and *The Thanksgiving over the Water* (306) serve as the prelude to the actual Baptism. There are seven prayers usually led by a member of the congregation and they take the place of The Prayers of the People at a typical Sunday Eucharist. Each prayer focuses on a specific dimension of the candidate's life after the ceremony: *deliver them from the way of sin and death, open their hearts to your grace and truth, fill them with your Holy Spirit, keep them in the faith and in your Church, teach them to love others, send them out to give witness, bring them your peace and glory.*

These are powerful prayers hand crafted by the founders of our Church through the power of the -Holy Spirit. They are prayers which should be prayed for every Christian and if Baptism is present tense then they are prayers that are needed not only at the time of the ceremony, but every day of our lives as we are challenged with the temptations of the world. The verbs of these seven prayers are: *delivering, opening, filling, keeping, teaching, sending, and bringing.* These are powerful, present tense verbs which are offered for a powerful, present tense Baptism.

The way we pray reflects what we believe; *lex orandi, lex credenda,* which is an ancient Christian principle and means, *the law of prayer is the law of belief(1).* In other words, if you listen to the way you pray, you will better understand what you believe. One of the reasons our **Book of Common Prayer** is revised from time to time is because our prayers have to be updated. Our prayers have to be updated because what we know and believe about God is constantly moving forward. There are many of our elderly congregants who love the 1928

Edition of our Prayer Book. There is richness and beauty in the '28 Prayer Book and it stood for a long time until it was updated by The 1979 Edition of The Prayer Book. That is a time span of 50 years. The Church's knowledge about God, relationship with God, and prayers to God had changed during those 50 years. You do not pray the same way you prayed 50 years ago, probably even 5 years ago, and so our prayers must reflect what we believe and hopefully, what we believe has drawn us closer to the truth of Jesus Christ.

The Prayers for the Candidate are a reflection of *The Five Difficult Questions* which follow The Apostles' Creed. To have any hope of fulfilling these five questions, to maintain the new Baptismal Covenant and The Reconciliation of a Penitent established by God with His people, the candidate will need the prayerful support of those who are witnessing the Baptism. We cannot live into our Baptism by ourselves. John Donne wrote, "No man is an island entire of itself. Every man is a piece of the continent. A part of the mainland." (2). John Donne became an Anglican priest and served as the Dean of St. Paul's Cathedral, London. He understood the importance of a Church community and the support that such a community provides. Offering our prayerful support is often times the only thing we can do, but it is by far the most powerful thing we can do.

The Prayers for the Candidate are reflected in the letter that Paul writes to the Christians in Colossae on the occasion of their newly found faith,

"For this reason, since the day we heard it, we have not ceased praying for you and asking that you may be filled with the knowledge of God's will in all spiritual wisdom and understanding, so that you may lead lives worthy of the Lord,

fully pleasing to him, as you bear fruit in every good work and as you grow in the knowledge of God," (Col. 1: 9,10).

The Thanksgiving over the Water (p. 306) is a prayer written by the Holy Spirit and has been part of The Rite of Baptism since the first **Book of Common Prayer** in 1549 (3). Every time I pray this prayer, I am filled with awe of The History of Salvation. It has its roots in the Spirit hovering over the water at creation (Gn. 1: 2), The Crossing of the Red Sea (Exodus 14), Moses striking the rock to provide water in the desert (Exodus 17), the crossing of the Jordan River into the Promised Land (Joshua 3), the ministry of John the Baptist (Mark 1), the Baptism of Jesus (Mark 1), The Samaritan Woman at the Well (John 4), Jesus' discussion about Baptism with Nicodemus (John 3), the fishermen (John 21), and Jesus' cry on the cross, "I am thirsty," (John 19:28).

The first person I ever baptized was a vibrant young man 75 years old. I asked him why he waited so long to be baptized. He explained that he always wanted to be baptized in the Jordan River, but he was never able to make it to the Holy Land and it seemed as though he was not going to be able to go any time soon. He understood the spiritual connection of such holy water and the role that the Jordan has had in Salvation History. Not to wait any longer, we decided that he would be baptized on Pentecost Sunday using regular holy water. At least the date would hold great significance.

A week before his Baptism, a friend of mine who had just returned from a trip to Israel and who knew nothing about the 75 year old man, gave me a small vile of water from the Jordan River! It was one of the most God awesome things I have ever experienced. Needless to say, I used the water from the Jordan River for his Baptism. As the expression goes, "If you can't come to Church, the Church will come to you." Praise God! Thank You, Jesus!

It is an awesome thing to be so connected to Salvation History. It is an awesome God Who has pieced together the salvation of the world using this thread of water. It is now our turn. We are honored and privileged to be a part of it. This is nothing to take for granted. It is ours to cherish. All of Salvation History comes into *The Blessing of the Water*. Abraham, Moses, and all of the prophets are watching. John the Baptist is watching. The Samaritan woman is watching. Nicodemus is watching. The fishermen are watching. The Communion of the Saints has gathered around the font. I always wish that moment would not end. It is disturbing to think that there are people in the pew looking at their watches and inwardly gasping, "Oh no, another Baptism!"

The water is then blessed (p. 307). It is now holy water. Holy water is used for Holy Baptism. We pray the Holy Spirit into the water, "…that those who here are cleansed from sin and born again may continue forever in the risen life of Jesus Christ our Savior." This is so holy. I mentioned in Section III: The Baptismal Vows, there is a series of six questions asked of the parents and godparents (p. 302). The first three are questions of renunciation, but the fourth question asks, "Do you turn to Jesus Christ and accept Him as your Savior?" I said at that time that water is the main symbol of Baptism, but "turn" is the main word. Praying the Spirit into the water for the cleansing of sin and rebirth in Christ is the core of this turn. This is the whole purpose of Holy Baptism. It is a holy thing when a life turns from sin and toward Jesus Christ. The thread of water used by God in The History of Salvation now sits in the font and is ready to be poured over the candidate.

I knew at six years old that I wanted to be a priest. While all of my friends wanted to be policemen and firemen, I knew God was calling me to be a priest. I was raised Roman Catholic and attended Roman Catholic schools my entire life. Early in my senior year in high school, my faculty advisor initiated the process of applying to the seminary. One of the initial steps was to be interviewed by the bishop.

This particular bishop had the reputation of being mean and grouchy. On the day of the interview, I began the 75 mile drive from my home to his office in Miami and I was scared to death. By the time I arrived and was greeted by his secretary, I was nervous as a cat. She escorted me into his office and explained that the bishop was in another meeting and that he would be with me shortly.

It was a very plush office. There was a big mahogany desk, thick pile carpeting, and large leather chairs. In the corner sat an old grandfather clock which ticked away the seconds of what seemed to be an eternity. But as I looked around, I noticed that the walls were practically bare. There were no diplomas or certificates. There were no pictures of him being consecrated a bishop, or him with other bishops. If he had ever met a cardinal or perhaps even the pope, there were certainly no signs of it hanging on his walls. The only thing on any of his walls was a modestly framed document mounted directly above his large leather swivel chair behind his desk. It was too small to read from my vantage point. But the longer I sat there, the more curious I became, and the more I felt the call by God to get up and check it out. It was God calling, right?

When the clock struck half past the hour, meaning that I had been waiting for 30 minutes, I finally mustered enough courage to walk over and look. It was still too difficult to read from the front of his desk so I walked around to the back of the desk, put my right knee into the seat of his chair straining my neck and positioned myself to read this rather small document. It was his Baptismal Certificate! I couldn't believe it! It was his Baptismal Certificate! I thought, "Well, even I have one of those!"

Just then the bishop walked through the door. When he looked at me, the brow on his forehead wrinkled and his eyes became piercing arrows, and I thought, "Oh my God, there is going to be a funeral! Someone may as well light the candles." I was speechless. My heart was ready to jump out of my throat. But when he began making sense of what was happening, the contortions on his face relaxed, his eyes warmed, and I think he might have even smiled. "That's my Baptismal Certificate," he said. And then it occurred to me, how could he do anything mean and nasty in the presence of his Baptismal Certificate?

That initiated a lengthy discussion about Baptism until the clocked chimed half past the next hour. We talked about Baptism for almost an hour. We talked about the priesthood about fifteen minutes, and even less than that about being a bishop. The interview was then over, he gave me his verbal stamp of approval, and I was on my way home. I realized that my initial impression of him was totally wrong. I came to know him as a very nice man, a man of God whom I had quickly grown to respect and admire, for it was in that conversation that I began to understand the significance of it all and I bring that conversation into every one I have with anyone who sits in front of me seeking to be baptized. That conversation began a lifelong journey into the true nature of Baptism and has intensified in my heart the necessity of accepting Jesus Christ as my Lord and Savior. I thank God for that hour. And as I stare at the holy water sitting in the font ready to be poured, I often think of a certain mean and grouchy bishop and a small certificate hanging on the wall of a very plush office.

The bishop was fulfilling his role of not only baptizing, but also of ordaining priests who continue the command by Jesus to make disciples. And even though I left the Roman Catholic seminary, I was eventually ordained by an Episcopal bishop whose sacramental role is the same. We are not baptized Roman Catholic or Episcopal or Methodist or Lutheran, but we are baptized Christian. The Rite of Holy Baptism opens with Paul's words to the Ephesians, *"There is one body and one Spirit, just as you were called to the one hope of your calling, one Lord, one faith, one Baptism, one God and Father of all, who is above all and through all and in all,"* (4: 4-6).

As the water is thrice poured over the head of the one being baptized, the baptizer announces, "N., I baptize you in the Name of the Father, and of the Son, and of the Holy Spirit. *Amen.* " (**BCP,** 307). Another Christian is brought into the Family of God. Another sinner repents. Another turn is made. The Church Community adds another member. Sunday attendance has just increased by one. The Holy Spirit has another heart in whom to dwell. The Body of Christ has one more heartbeat. The vine has another shoot. The Kingdom has one more future resident. And the Communion of the Saints has further reason to rejoice.

Conditional Baptism and Emergency Baptism

(**BCP.** 313)

What happens if an individual is uncertain whether or not he/she has been baptized? If the parents have died, or for some unknown reason there is some doubt whether the ceremony has ever taken place or there is some doubt that the Baptism was in the name of the Trinity, then what happens? **The Prayer Book** makes a provision for this. The candidate would go through the same Baptismal Preparation as anyone seeking to be baptized and the ceremony would be the same, but at the time to pour the water the baptizer states, "*If you have not already been baptized*, N., I baptize you in the Name of the Father, and of the Son, and of the Holy Spirit."

In the case of an emergency such as an automobile accident, a baby still born, or any unforeseen tragedy, any baptized person may administer Baptism simply by pouring the water three times and using the Name of the Trinity.

The Anointing

I grew up loving television shows about the Old West. Cowboys and camp fires always struck a chord with me. My favorite was *Bonanza*. It was on Sunday nights and when we did not have school on Monday, it was always a treat to be able to stay up and watch it.

The Cartwrights were cattle ranchers; herds of cattle that they would bring to The Ponderosa and grow to maturity. Like other ranchers, they had their own special brand that distinguished their calves from those of other ranches. Little Joe would occasionally load up a buck board with bob wire fencing, fence posts, and tools and would ride the perimeter of the ranch to make sure there were no holes in the fence for the cattle to escape. Of course, he always found one or two, some from deteriorating fence posts that allowed the cattle to stray, but some parts of the fence which had been cut by thieves who stole some of the herd. While the former necessitated a search to find the missing ones, round them up and bring them back to the ranch, the latter always produced a conflict between the good guys and the bad guys. The brand on the hip of the cattle was always the tell-tale sign and even though the thieves would attempt to alter the brand, the original one was always plain to see.

The Anointing with Chrism has the same spiritual effect. The baptizer uses the chrism and traces the sign of the cross on the forehead of the one being baptized using the words, "N., you are sealed by the Holy Spirit in Baptism and marked as Christ's own forever. *Amen."* (**BCP,** 308). The baptized is sealed and marked; branded so to speak. And even though the oil on the forehead will eventually be washed away, the eternal mark on the soul remains forever. The spirits see this mark and instantly know that this one belongs to Christ.

However, because of free will, baptized people still stray, and like a thief, the evil one will try to steal away the anointed. Jesus is constantly riding the range to reclaim those who belong to Him and to return to the ranch those who have crossed beyond the perimeter of the Kingdom. This is the image we are given in The Parable of the Good Shepherd (Jn. 10: 11-18). Jesus uses the biblical image of a shepherd, but He is constantly searching for those who are lost. *"I am the Good Shepherd. The good shepherd lays down his life for the sheep. I know my sheep and my sheep know me, just as the Father knows me and I know the Father,"* (10: 11,14). The core of spiritual warfare is Jesus' conflict with the thief. The thief is constantly trying to steal and Jesus is constantly riding the range because Baptism is present tense.

The anointing of the Holy Spirit with chrism makes all of the water in our body holy. As mentioned from the very beginning, humans are 80% water. The anointing makes us living fountains of holiness. As we lose some of this water through perspiration and evaporation, the water needs to be replenished. When we consume water through the course of the day, the new water mixes with the present water and becomes just as holy; the new water does not "water down" the holy water we presently have, rather, the holy water we presently have consumes the new water to make it just as holy. It does not lose its potency of holiness. If after blessing the water in the font I were to add more water, then all of it has the same holiness. It is not like adding more water to your glass of ice tea because it is too strong and you want more water and less tea. On the contrary, the consumption of secular water completely takes on the properties of the holy water within us. Could it be that when doctors and health advocates tell us to drink plenty of water throughout the day that they are giving us spiritual direction as well?

Receiving the Newly Baptized

(BCP, 308)

The Church has moved away from private Baptisms, those where only the family is present. The Prayer Book tells us that Holy Baptism is appropriately administered on Sunday or on a major Feast Day within the context of Holy Eucharist (p. 298). Baptism and community go hand in hand. The baptized is welcomed into the Family of God, the community vows its support, and the community is strengthened by increased membership in the faith.

The baptizer initiates this welcome,

"Let us welcome the newly baptized."

The congregation responds,

We receive you into the household of God. Confess the faith of Christ crucified, proclaim his resurrection, and share with us in his eternal priesthood."

The Church where I serve is growing rapidly. Our ratio of Baptisms to Burials is nearly 2-1. I tell the people, "Do not say, 'Oh no, another Baptism.' Rather, to say, 'Oh yea, another Baptism!'" Because each Baptism is our witness to the faith and each Baptism proclaims the resurrection of Jesus Christ. If they were not so faithful and committed and alive with the Holy Spirit then we would not have any Baptisms at all. It's really their fault.

The Rite of Baptism is now finished, but the journey has just begun. Like a wedding where the ceremony and reception lasts a day, but the marriage lasts a lifetime, so too, the Baptismal Ceremony and reception will soon be over, but the challenge of living a Christian life has just taken its first step. Hopefully the newly baptized will find daily joy in the resurrection knowing that the Kingdom lies ahead, and yet find great comfort during times of hardship and even despair. This can only happen within a community. The community is needed to learn about the Lord; to worship Him in the Eucharist when we can receive His Body and Blood, to help study the scriptures, to pray together, to celebrate, and to mourn and grieve together. The community will become an important part in all of this. It defeats the purpose of Baptism to become disconnected from the community. No one can do all of this alone. No one is an island all by itself. Each person is part of the mainland.

When you go to Church, do not think that you are alone. Even though you may have traveled there by yourself, once you arrive, you are in the midst of a community, the living, breathing Family of God. Look around. You are surrounded by your brothers and sisters in Christ, sons and daughters of God, the Father. Each one has been created by the Master, baptized into the life of His Son, and anointed with His Holy Spirit. You are one of them. You are one of us. And we are all pilgrims making our way to the Kingdom.

Questions

1. Jesus instructs His disciples to make disciples of all nations and baptize them in the name of the Trinity. Where does this instruction by Jesus rank in your list of life's priorities?
2. Lex orandi, lex credenda. The law of prayer is the law of belief. Have you ever listened to the way you pray? Does it truly reflect what you believe?
3. Do you understand that when you enter into some illicit activity that you take the anointed water of your Baptism with you?
4. No one is an island. Do you feel connected to your Church Community?
5. Do you think of yourself as being anointed?
6. Have you ever felt the evil one at work in your life?
7. When you arrive at Church and discover that there is a Baptism, do you say to yourself, "Oh no, another Baptism!" Or do you say to yourself, "Oh yea, another Baptism!"?

Section X: Overriding Questions

The Big Picture

1. Compare your attitude regarding Baptism before you read this booklet to after you read it.
2. Is Jesus Christ your Lord and Savior?
3. Have you made "the turn"?
4. Are you ready to make the commitment that comes along with being baptized?
5. This is our turn in Salvation History. What responsibility do you have?
6. Which of the six questions in The Baptismal Covenant is most difficult for you to accept?
7. Baptism is present tense. What are your biggest spiritual struggles on a daily basis?

End Notes

Introduction
1. Constitution and Canons of the Episcopal Church; Canon III.9.5 (3) *Preparing Persons for Baptism*

Section I: Baptism Is Present Tense
1. *100 Very Cool Facts About The Human Body:* Wikipedia. 2008
2. **The Winning Attitude,** John Maxwell. 1993
3. **Virtue and Vice In Everyday Life,** Christina Sommers and Fred Sommers. 2004.

Section II: Baptism is the Sign of a New Covenant
1. *Abraham:* **The Oxford Companion to the Bible,** Metzger and Coogan. Oxford University Press. 1993.
2,3,4. *Circumcision:* Wikipedia. 2012
5. *Job:* **Jerome Biblical Commentary,** R.A.F. MacKenzie, S.J.; Prentice-Hall, Inc. 1968.
6. cf: Acts 10: 44-48

Section III: The Baptismal Vows
1. **The Cost of Discipleship,** Dietrich Bonhoeffer. 1937
2. *Sin:* **The Oxford Campion to the Bible,** Metzger and Coogan. 1993.
3. *Faith:* ibid.

Section IV: Spirit of Adoption
1. *Abba:* **Nelson's New Illustrated Bible Dictionary,** Ronald F. Youngblood, Ed. 1995.
2. *The Articles of Religion:* Article XXVIII, "Of The Lord's Supper," (**BCP,** 873).

Section V: The Baptism of Jesus
1. **Christus Veritus,** William Temple. 1939.
2. Ibid
3. *The Articles of Religion:* Article II, "Of The Word or Son of God, Which Was Made Very Man," (**BCP,** 868).

Section VI: Gifts of the Holy Spirit
1. Cf: Heb. 2:4 ff, 1 Cor. 12:1 ff, Rom. 12:6 ff.
2. Cf: *Finding Your Spiritual Gifts,* C. Peter Wagner. 2005.

Section VII: Death and Resurrection
1. Cf: 2 Ti. 1:8, Heb. 10:32, Rom. 5:3, 2 Ti. 3:11

Section VIII: The Baptismal Covenant
1. *The Apostles' Creed:* Wikipedia. 2008
2. **Commentary on the American Prayer Book,** Marion Hatchett. 1995
3. *St. Augustine:* **Lives of the Saints**; Catholic Book Publishing Co, 1993.
4. *Martin Buber:* Wikipedia. 2008

Section IX: The Baptism
1. *Lex Orandi, Lex Crendenda:* Wikipedia, 2008
2. *John Donne:* Wikipedia, 2008
3. **Commentary on the American Prayer Book**, Marion Hatchett. 1995.

CPSIA information can be obtained
at www.ICGtesting.com
Printed in the USA
BVHW041830021120
592351BV00020B/256

9 781498 416177